PSY

THE LANGUAGE OF DECISION

THE LANGUAGE OF DECISION

An Essay in Prescriptivist Ethical Theory

John Ibberson

MACMILLAN

First published 1986

Published by
THE MACMILLAN PRESS LTD
Houndmills, Basingstoke, Hampshire RG21 2XS
and London
Companies and representatives
throughout the world

Printed in Hong Kong

British Library Cataloguing in Publication Data
Ibberson, John
The language of decision: an essay in
prescriptivist ethical theory.
1. Language and ethics
I. Title
170'.14   BJ44
ISBN 0–333–40661–3

Contents

v

Preface

This is a book advocating prescriptivism as a theory of ethics. Pre-scriptivism is not here defended as an empirical hypothesis about what we actually mean by our evaluative vocabulary, for probably no consistent theory could accommodate everyone's linguistic intuitions. Instead, this work examines the logical consequences of both a prescriptive and a descriptive use of ethical terms, and concludes that the prescriptive use is sufficient to express all that it is coherent to say. The only *facts* required for ethics are the ordinary empirical facts on which we base our value judgements, together with the truths of logic. We do not need to affirm the existence of non-natural ethical facts, since such affirmations do no intelligible work that is not already carried out by statements of empirical fact and sentences in the imperative and optative moods. And if value judgements were statements of certain natural or empirical facts then no one could ever be logically committed, upon accepting a value judgement, to thinking he had any reason at all for acting in one way rather than another. Such a logical commitment can be secured only if evaluative terms are used prescriptively.

I wish to express my sincere thanks to Professor R. M. Hare and Dr M. J. Lockwood of Oxford, and to Dr P. S. Mamo, formerly of the University of Calgary, for many enjoyable and profitable discussions.

J. R. I.
Calgary

Introduction

This essay is a defence of certain insights of prescriptivist ethical theory. I do not defend it as a correct description of what we actually mean by our evaluative vocabulary, but as showing us certain things which we all wish to say and would be unable to say with evaluative words if the value judgements they are used to express were simply statements of fact which were either true or false. The principal claim of this book is that if value judgements were capable of being true then they could have no logically necessary relevance to any choice of conduct. This is because no prescriptive conclusion can follow logically from any set of purely factual premises except in the degenerate case where the truth of the premises makes it impossible not to satisfy the prescriptive conclusion.

(i) If, for instance, in saying that some action is morally right or wrong, we are describing that action as having certain properties, then those properties are either identical with or distinct from the empirically observable features of the action on the basis of which we make our moral appraisal. If the moral and empirical features are distinct then it is impossible that we should know whether all (or even any) actions with particular empirical features also have the alleged moral characteristics. The correlation between these features could never be established inductively since a necessary characteristic of an inductive generalization is that each of the correlated features be observable independently of the other; and everyone agrees that we cannot know whether an action is right or wrong without first being aware of the empirical features which 'make' it right or wrong. The empirical features we observe do not even provide a reason for postulating unobservable moral characteristics, since the presence of those characteristics could not explain the observable features in the way that postulating the existence of electrons might explain what is observed in the Wilson cloud chamber: for, it is not because an action is wrong that it has certain empirical features, rather it is because it has those features that it is wrong.

1

On the other hand, if the moral and empirical features are identical then a difficulty arises similar to Frege's problem about the Morning Star and the Evening Star: if the moral property M is identical with the empirical feature E, then how can the statement 'M = E' differ from the uninformative tautology 'M = M'? Frege's solution was to say that the sense of any expression used to call something the Morning Star was different from the sense of expressions used to call it the Evening Star, although both expressions had the same reference; and to know the sense of such an expression was to have a set of instructions for identifying its referent. Consequently, if two people who are correctly following their instructions identify the referent of an expression with different objects, then they must be following different instructions, i.e. they must be attaching different senses to the expression. Their apparent disagreement is really just a verbal misunderstanding, which is to be resolved by making a linguistic decision to adopt one sense or the other.

In any case, the question concerning the identity of moral and empirical properties has no bearing whatever on any practical question about what to do. For, either the empirical features of an action provide a conclusive and overriding reason not to perform that action, or they do not. Suppose they do. Then it does not matter whether those features also make the action wrong, since the wrongness of an action can provide no *more* reason not to do it than the empirical features that make it wrong. Suppose they do not. Then again it does not matter whether they make the action wrong; for even if they did make it wrong, its wrongness could not provide an overriding reason not to do it if the empirical features that make it wrong do not also provide such a reason.

(ii) In order to defend these claims it is necessary to investigate the relation between sincerely assenting to a prescription and intending to do what it prescribes, and to argue that if there are any logical relations between statements of fact and prescriptions then they are captured only in what is called the Logic of Satisfaction.

Just as sincere assent to a statement of fact requires a belief that the statement is true, so sincere assent to a prescription (or to an 'imperative' in the generic sense) addressed to ourselves requires an intention to do what is prescribed. A universal prescription is described (R. M. Hare, *The Language of Morals*, p. 188) as one which entails imperative sentences in all the persons as well as in all the tenses. This raises a problem about, among other things, past-tense imperatives: to issue a universal prescription is to prescribe that certain things happen in the past as well as in the present and future. And it is not clear what sense can be attached to the notion of intending that something happen in the past (especially something that is known not to have happened). There is no point in trying to justify the notion of a past-tense prescription by analogy with the use of imaginary numbers in mathematics and physics since the notion of an imaginary *number* (as opposed to an operator or a matrix) is itself incoherent. This problem can be avoided by observing the distinction between the kind of wanting 'of which the primitive sign is trying-to-get' and idle wishing: these two kinds of wishes will be expressed by sentences in the imperative and optative moods respectively. Then moral judgements could at least coherently be thought to entail imperative sentences in *some* of the persons and some of the tenses, and optative sentences in the rest.

A theory about the logic of prescriptions must have a way of characterizing what logical relations there are, if any, between statements of fact and prescriptions. It will be useless to suppose that a statement entails a prescription just in case it is logically impossible for the statement to be true and the prescription false; since it is logically impossible for any prescription to be false (or true) it would follow that any statement entailed every prescription. The only plausible notion of entailment here is one according to which a statement entails a prescription *only if* it is logically impossible for the statement to be true and the prescription unsatisfied, e.g. 'Caesar is dead; therefore, don't kill Caesar'. But in that case, if moral judgements were statements of fact then 'It is morally wrong to do X' could not logically entail 'Do not do X', and 'It is morally wrong not to do X' could not entail 'Do X', unless it were logically impossible to do what was wrong. Moral judgements can either follow logically from statements of fact, in which case they do not entail prescriptions, or they can logically entail prescriptions, in which case they do not follow from statements of fact.

(iii) No fact can provide a logically conclusive reason to do something unless a statement of that fact logically entails a prescription to do that thing; and this cannot happen unless it is logically impossible not to do what is prescribed when the statement is true. But a fact can still provide a sufficient reason to do something even if does not constitute a *logically* conclusive reason. This is explained by showing that it is not a fact *about* any state of affairs that it constitutes a reason to do something, since to *say* that it is a reason is not to *state* any fact about it; it is to say 'Other things being equal, do X because this state of affairs obtains'. Similarly, evidence consists of reasons to believe something, and to say that a set of facts constitutes strong evidence in support of a certain conclusion is to say 'Other things being equal, believe strongly that this conclusion is true, because of those facts'.

If someone asks 'What shall I do?' we can report his question in oratio obliqua by saying that he asked what he should do. If he is told 'Do not do X' and asks 'Why not?', he is asking why he should not do X; and to answer his question is to say why he shouldn't. But when he is told not to do X he is not being informed of any fact, and consequently when he asks 'Why not?' he is not asking for the explanation of any fact (as he would be if, when told 'The bomb did not explode', he asked 'Why not?'). Therefore to say *that* he should not do X is not to state any fact; it is simply to tell him not *to* do it. The word 'should' is being used here simply as the past tense of 'shall'. Using direct speech we can report: God said 'Thou *shalt* not eat' of the tree of the knowledge of good and evil. Using indirect speech God can report his own utterance by saying 'I commanded thee that thou *shouldest* not eat of it.'

There is a persistent tendency to confuse explanations and justifications, and consequently to suppose that no one can have a reason to do anything unless he has a desire to do it. A fact may *be* a reason why someone should perform a certain action (no matter what his desires happen to be) even though he will not *agree* that it is a reason unless that fact shows him how performing that action will get him something he wants. But the mere fact that he does not agree that it is a reason does not show that it is not a reason. Nevertheless a desire is always necessary if a factual belief is to succeed in motivating an action. Here, the word 'desire' means just 'whatever it is that enables beliefs to motivate action'; a desire is a dispositional state whose underlying neurological basis may be unknown but which is activated by the acquisition of factual beliefs. This does not trivialize the claim that a desire must be present before beliefs will motivate action; the important point is that desires and beliefs are *distinct* kinds of mental states, even though referring to a disposition as simply a 'desire' does not *explain* how the beliefs can motivate an action. Gravitational mass is similarly a dispositional state whose underlying basis we do not know; and the word 'gravity' means just 'whatever it is that makes objects fall when left unsupported.' Thus even though referring to this disposition as simply 'gravitational mass' does not *explain* why unsupported objects fall, nevertheless having this disposition is something *distinct* from actually falling or being left unsupported.

Without gravitational mass, leaving an object unsupported will not *cause* it to fall (although it may fall spontaneously); and without a desire, beliefs will not *motivate* a person to perform an action (although he may perform it anyway, for no reason at all).

(iv) Since this book was the result of a conversion away from Ethical Naturalism it is useful and appropriate to explain what is initially appealing and what is ultimately unsatisfactory in Naturalism. The Open-Question Argument was an attempt to show that evaluative properties must be distinct from empirical properties since evaluative words do not mean the same as words for empirical properties. Yet the fact that two names or descriptions are not synonymous does not show that they are not names or two descriptions of the same thing. Suppose the name 'Xerxes I' means 'the Persian king who lost the Battle of Salamis' and the name 'Ahasuerus' means 'the Persian king who married Esther'; the mere fact that 'Xerxes I' does not *mean* the same as 'Ahasuerus' does not show that Xerxes I cannot *be* the same person as Ahasuerus. Some further argument is therefore needed to explain why the fact that the expression 'being good' does not mean the same as 'being pleasant' shows that being good is not the same property as being pleasant.

Now part of this further argument consists of pointing out the features of proper names, definite descriptions and natural kind terms which enable them to express necessary identity statements, and showing that these features are not possessed by evaluative terms. For instance, wrong actions do not form a natural kind like gold or water whose 'real essence' or underlying, hidden constitution explains its outward, manifest appearance or 'nominal essence'; an action's having the unobserved property of wrongness does not explain why it had the obvious property of being a punishment of the innocent, rather the action's being a case of punishing the innocent is the reason why it was wrong. It is possible to explain how proper names can be used to express synthetic, necessary identity statements if a certain account is adopted of what it is to *refer* to things. But if wrongness is a property of actions then it is not clear that we could ever refer to that property as we can refer to the king of Persia who married Esther; even if, for the sake of logic, we should be forced to admit the real existence of such objects as events and actions, we do not have to admit the existence of properties of those actions. And if there not only *are not* but *cannot be* such things as properties then it is difficult to see how we can refer to them.

Defenders of Ethical Naturalism *de re* maintain that evaluative properties are identical with certain empirical features even though the words for these properties are not synonymous, and so they claim to have avoided the Open-Question Argument. But sooner or later they must identify the *sense* of their evaluative terms with the sense of some empirical descriptions if they are to have instructions which will lead them to the empirical properties which they claim are identical with the evaluative properties. And if two naturalists disagree about which instructions to follow they must simply be attaching different senses to the same evaluative term, and then they are involved in a mere verbal misunderstanding rather than a genuine ethical disagreement.

(v) Finally, it is apt to be thought that the version of prescriptivism which I expound is a species of subjectivism since it denies objective truth to claims about what we should do and why we should do it. If this is meant to be a criticism of the theory then it is an empty one, since the notion of an 'objective prescription' or an 'intrinsically prescriptive fact' is incoherent. There can be no facts which have an intrinsic capacity to motivate anyone aware of them, and this has nothing to do with the existence of God. Even if God made us such as to be motivated to fulfil his purposes once we are aware of certain facts, this is only a contingent fact about the way God made us. He might have made us differently.

The mere fact that we were created for some purpose does not entail any prescription to pursue the fulfilment of that purpose. The claim 'God created us for purpose P' will entail 'Pursue purpose P' only if this claim means something like 'A being whose purposes are to be fulfilled has created us for purpose P'; but to say that someone's purposes *are to be* fulfilled is not in this instance to make a prediction but to issue a prescription.

Yet none of this has any tendency to show that values are subjective in the sense that 'all value judgements are equally good'. For, this is itself a prescription to value everything equally, and as such cannot follow from any statement of fact; in particular, it cannot follow from any prescriptivist theory of ethics.

1 The Relevance of Morality to Practice

Philosophers have long concerned themselves with the question whether moral judgements, and evaluative judgements in general, ever follow logically from statements of fact. If they do, then of course they are themselves a species of factual judgement and hence are either true or false and can be known as easily as the facts by which they are entailed. But if they are more like commands or other prescriptions, if for instance 'X is wrong' means simply 'Don't anyone ever do X', then they are neither true nor false, do not in the same sense follow logically from statements of fact, and there is no question of knowing whether an action is right or wrong, in the sense of 'knowing' according to which only what is true can be known. Now, I have no idea whether calling an action right or wrong is to state a fact about it or to issue a prescription. But if an action's being right or wrong is a *non*-empirical fact about it then I do not see how its moral status can ever be known to us, or how its empirical features can be relevant in determining this status. If on the other hand its rightness or wrongness is an empirical fact about it, then we have to determine which fact, of all those we already know about it, the sentences which express moral judgements are used to state. And this seems to be a question better left to those interested in semantics.

ETHICAL INTUITIONISM BASED ON INDUCTIVE GENERALIZATION

It is commonly said that most of us are perfectly able to distinguish right actions from wrong, at least in the obvious cases. But if the accounts concerning the nature of right and wrong given by some of the people who say this were correct, then this would be impossible. Certain Intuitionists, for instance, held that right and wrong, good and bad, were genuine properties of things; but they were convinced

7

that the *words* 'right' and 'wrong', 'good' and 'bad', were not synonymous with any other words standing for empirically observable
properties, and from this they inferred that the properties themselves
which the evaluative words stood for were not identical with any
empirical properties. Now some of them allowed that everything
having a given evaluative property might also have a particular
empirical feature, and others went so far as to admit that things
possessed evaluative properties only because they also had particular
empirical features, but they all insisted that the evaluative properties
were entirely distinct from the empirical properties.

The view that the evaluative features of a thing are consequential
properties, that is, different from its empirical features but dependent
or 'supervenient' upon them, does not of course entail which observable characteristics are those by virtue of which things have their
evaluative features. But in practice Intuitionists often turned out to
be anti-Utilitarians. They typically held, for instance, that it is always
wrong knowingly to punish an innocent person, no matter how much
good it accomplishes or how much suffering it averts; it is wrong
simply because the person is innocent, although his innocence is an
empirical feature which is no part of the wrongness of punishing him.

This raised a problem about moral knowledge. The fact that a
person has not committed the crime for which he is to be punished is
one that can be established or supported by empirical investigation.
But if the wrongness of punishing him is a fact about the action which
is entirely distinct from any fact which is open to empirical confirmation, then how do we know that those actions which consist in
punishing the innocent are *ever* attended with the further property of
being wrong? The answer of the Intuitionists was to postulate a
special faculty of intuition which gave us 'direct insight' to the
evaluative nature of things and provided 'immediate awareness' of
those properties which eluded detection by ordinary empirical
methods. And it is clear that if the fact that it would be wrong to
punish a person is ever to be inferred from the completely different
fact that he is innocent, then some such answer is required in order to
explain how we acquired a knowledge of the validity of the inference
in the first place.

We cannot base the inference on inductive generalization, as
though every case of punishing the innocent so far observed had also
been found to be wrong, which would render it only highly probable
that future instances would be wrong as well. For, as P. F. Strawson
has pointed out,[1] in order to establish by induction that the posses-

sion by something of one feature is a reliable indication of the presence of another feature, we must be able to detect each of them independently of the other. We think that a person's having a fever and breaking out in spots of a given description are reliable indicators that he is infected with a certain virus, and we can test this conjecture because the evidence for the presence of the virus is independent of the evidence for the prescence of the symptoms; the laboratory technician does not have to know whether the patient has already developed a fever and broken out in spots in order to determine whether a sample of his blood contains the virus.

If we supposed that the facts cited by the Intuitionist provided merely a reliable indication that the punishment would be wrong, but did not actually constitute its wrongness, then we should be able to test this supposition by finding out whether an action is wrong without knowing any of the indicators which are distinct from but merely point to its wrongness. If its wrongness is no part of its being a case of punishing the innocent, in the way that being female is part of being a woman, but is something extra that is always supposed to accompany such punishments, then in at least some cases we should be able to determine whether the correlation holds by detecting the wrongness without being aware of what sort of punishment it is, or even whether it is a case of punishment at all. In fact, if the features of an action which constitute the reasons why it is wrong amount only to reliable indicators, then we ought to be able to tell whether it is wrong without knowing anything at all about it that could be a reason why it was wrong.

But this is obviously impossible, as every Intuitionist will admit. We have to know something about an act if we are to tell whether it is wrong. And in this respect the relation between the wrongness of an action and the features of it that make it wrong differs from the relation between the colour of an object and the sort of light it reflects which makes it that colour. It is true that the colour of an object is said to be supervenient upon features of it, such as the wave length of light reflected from it, which can be described in words not synonymous with any colour expressions; and this supervenience or dependence holds by virtue of the fact that a thing is the colour it is because of, e.g. the sort of light it reflects, and there can be no differences in colour without corresponding differences in the light reflected or in some other features describable in non-colour terms. But we can determine a thing's colour and the sort of light it reflects independently of each other; for the one you look at a photometer, for the other you look at the object itself. Now Intuitionists confess that you cannot know whether an action is right or wrong except by being aware of those other features which make it right or wrong.[2] But whatever feature it is that we have to know, the question that will immediately arise is how it could even provide evidence for the presence of the moral attribute if we can never establish an inductive correlation between the two by detecting each of them independently of the other.

Now of course there is a way in which one thing can provide evidence for the presence of another even when the other cannot be observed at all, let alone independently of the first. We are not always in as fortunate a position as the lab technician who can look through the microscope and actually see the virus. And even here our confidence that the image is not distorted, making the virus look disproportionately fatter or thinner than it really is, can only be as strong as our confidence in the optical theory of the microscope. In other cases the situation is worse. We cannot, for instance, observe electrons independently of observing other things which we take to be evidence for them, and it may be that there are some things we cannot observe directly even in principle. But in these cases the observations we do make provide evidence for the existence of the postulated entities because by supposing that they exist we can explain what we observe. We can explain why there is a trail of bubbles in the cloud chamber by supposing that an electron has just gone by, ionizing the gas molecules in its path which then form centres of condensation.

But explanation is precisely the feature that is lacking from the case where what we know about an act is supposed to provide evidence for the presence of other properties of a moral nature. For no one thinks that we can explain why an act was an example of punishing the innocent by supposing that it was wrong. This would be exactly backwards. It is not because it was wrong that it was a punishment of the innocent; it is because it was a punishment of the innocent that it was supposed to be wrong.

Now if the moral properties of an action cannot be independently correlated with its observable features, and do not explain the presence of these features, then either the moral properties are not really distinct from the observable ones on which they are said to be dependent or else we have no reason at all for supposing that actions ever have them.

Some have suggested that even without observation it is self-evident that the undetectable moral properties always accompany certain empirical features of actions.[3] Thus it is said to be self-evident that it is wrong to torture people just for fun, in the same way that it is self-evident that all three-sided figures have three angles. But this analogy will not do, for the crucial feature of the moral case is absent from the geometrical example: on the one hand, the wrongness is supposed to be a feature entirely distinct from the empirical property of being an act of torture whose only purpose is to amuse the torturer, while on the other hand the property of being a three-sided figure is identical with the property of being a three-angled figure. Obviously, for an end of one side to meet an end of another side is the same thing as their forming an angle; that is, their forming an angle is not anything over and above their meeting. If the other end of the first side meets an end of a third side, this constitutes a second angle; and if the remaining ends of the second and third sides meet they form a third angle. So the property of having three sides which meet in this way, and the property of having three angles, are not two different properties which are constantly conjoined by some mysterious necessity; they are one and the same property.

For any such analogy to be relevant it must have two features: the properties whose constant conjunction is alleged to be self-evident must really be distinct properties, and one of them must be empirically unobservable – unlike the angles and sides of a figure which can be counted independently. Richard Price suggested that our knowledge of right and wrong is like our knowledge that every event has a cause.[4] We can establish by observation that a certain event has occurred and was preceded by another; we can also observe that events of the first sort are invariably preceded by events of the second. What we cannot observe is that the earlier event caused the later one. The train of events as one follows the other is open to perception, but the necessary connections between events are invisible: as far as observation is concerned, a world in which every event has a cause is indistinguishable from a world in which events occur in the same sequence but no event causes or is caused by any other; they simply occur spontaneously.

Nevertheless, thought Price, all of us have the notion of cause and effect, and since we did not derive it from experience we must have within ourselves an independent source of concepts, which might also be the faculty that provides us with our notions of right and wrong.

He held that this very source of non-empirical concepts enabled us to perceive that every case of punishing the innocent or torturing people for fun was necessarily wrong, just as it revealed to us that every occurrence necessarily had a cause.

But it is difficult to see how it can reveal any such thing. Let our notions of causation or of right and wrong be as inate as possible; our mere possession of these notions does not guarantee that anything actually instantiates them. And if we cannot acquire the concept of a cause from experience then no experience can tell us whether any event ever falls under it; for if it could, then the same experience would be enough to supply us with the notion of causation itself, and then there would be no reason to suppose the idea of cause and effect to be innate.[5] But just as our having the concept of a necessary connection between events does not ensure that there is such a connection, so our having the notion of an undetectable, evaluative property which necessarily accompanies certain empirical features of actions does not show that there is such a property or that anything ever has it. And if we cannot know empirically that anything in the world corresponds to these notions, it is hard to see how we can know it at all.

TURNING MORAL DISAGREEMENT INTO VERBAL DISPUTE

These are the consequences of supposing that the rightness or wrong-ness of an action is a characteristic of it which is dependent upon, but no part of, the empirical features which make the action right or wrong. Others have thought that in order, for instance, to answer the question 'Why, or by virtue of what, is it wrong to punish the innocent?' we must cite a fact which actually constitutes the punish-ment's being wrong, and not a different fact which is just constantly conjoined with its wrongness. Of course the word 'make' can be interpreted causally or constitutively in different contexts: it might be appropriate in one context to say, for instance, that what makes someone a thief is the fact that he steals things, while in another context we are supposed to say that growing up in a deprived environment is what usually makes someone a thief. The first answer and not the second is appropriate when the question 'What makes some-one a thief?' means 'What is it for someone to be a thief?', and we are thereby invited to supply an identity statement such as 'To be a thief is the same as to steal things.'

This is apparently how Socrates interpreted such questions. When he asked what made a person virtuous he wanted to know what being virtuous consisted in, and not what causally explained how the characteristics which constituted virtue were acquired. In the *Meno* he argued that you had to know what virtue was before you could hope to find out how to acquire it. For unless you were able to identify independently the effect you were trying to explain, you could not even set out to investigate what brought it about.

But there are difficulties just as serious with this view as well. For if an action's being right or wrong were a fact about it, but not an additional fact over and above its having those empirical features which make it right or wrong, then it would seem that any moral disagreement in which the empirical facts are not in dispute must really be a verbal disagreement about which of these facts we are stating by calling it right or wrong. For example, utilitarians and deontologists regularly disagree about whether it could ever be right to punish a person, knowing that he was innocent. We may imagine two of them to have a specific case in mind where they both agree that the suffering to be inflicted on the innocent victim is less than the suffering that would result to others by not making an example of anyone. We are to suppose that they differ only in that the utilitarian holds that it would be right to impose the punishment in virtue of its consequences, while the deontologist says it would be wrong in virtue of the prisoner's innocence. Each of them acknowledges the fact which the other alleges the rightness or wrongness to consist in, but neither agrees that it consists in the fact which the other points out. Now it certainly seems to them that something more is at issue than simply the meanings of words. Yet how could that be, if the punishment's being right or wrong were a fact about it and, moreover, one which obtained solely by virtue of either the fact that it would be a case of punishing the innocent or the fact that it would be a case of preventing greater suffering to others, both of which they acknowledge?

Their situation seems very similar to that of two people disputing whether a dog succeeds in running 'around' a cow who pivots so as always to keep her horns facing towards him. One says he doesn't because he never gets behind her, and the other says he does because goes all around where she is standing. All that can be done to resolve such a dispute is to get each of them to understand what leads the other to say what he does. And since it is not a further fact whether the dog goes around the cow, in addition to his running around the spot where she stands but not getting behind her, it is clear that there is no real disagreement about what the dog actually does but only a linguistic dispute about which word is properly used to say what he does.[6]

Now the utilitarian and the deontologist both agree that the prisoner is innocent and that in this case punishing him would prevent greater suffering to others; they also agree that the action's being right or wrong consists in nothing more than these two facts about it. What then do they disagree about? Whatever feature of the act is singled out by the deontologist as that in which the wrongness consists, the utilitarian will certainly acknowledge it as a component in the punishment; and whatever feature the utilitarian points to as constituting the rightness of the punishment will also be recognized by the deontologist. So if there is still to be a genuine dispute between them each must think that convincing the other of the presence of the moral property is a task over and above convincing him that the punishment has the empirical feature which he nevertheless holds to be identical with the moral property. Thinking that it has the relevant moral characteristic C must be different from thinking that it has the empirical feature F, even though its having the one characteristic isn't anything different from its having the other.

But the only way in which a thought identifying something with characteristic C can differ from a thought identifying the same thing with feature F, when C and F are identical, is by containing different concepts. Thus, the property of being the cube root of 64 is the same as the property of being the square of 2, although the thought that something is the cube root of 64 involves the concept of multiplying a number by itself *three* times, which is not involved in the thought that it equals the square of 2. The property of being one metre long is the same as the property of being 39.37 inches long, although the second thought involves the notion of an inch while the first one does not. The two thoughts contain different notions of the same property just as two sentences may contain different identifying descriptions of the same thing.

If the thought that an action is wrong contains concepts not involved in the thought that it has a certain empirical feature, even when this feature is what constitutes wrongness, then we must determine which these extra concepts are; for unless we can do that we will be unable to tell whether the moral property that falls under the one notion is really identical with the empirical property that falls under the other. Thus, the thought that an object is the Morning Star is different from the thought that it is the Evening Star because the idea or notion of the Morning Star contains concepts not involved in the notion of the Evening Star. The one contains the concept of appearing first in the evening sky, while the other involves the concept of disappearing last from the morning sky. Once we know which empirical concepts are involved in the two notions we can set out to discover whether the object falling under the one notion, by virtue of appearing first in the evening sky, is the same as the object falling under the other notion, by virtue of disappearing last from the morning sky as well. But if there is disagreement about which concepts make up the notions of moral wrongness, or of the Morning and Evening Stars, then there will also be disagreement about how to find out whether the Morning and Evening Stars are identical or which empirical property is identical with wrongness.

MENO'S PARADOX

This is precisely the problem encountered in Plato's *Meno*. In the *Euthyphro* Socrates had asked for a definition of piety so that, looking to it as a standard, he could tell which actions were pious and which were not. If he knew which empirical features were the defining characteristics of a pious action, and also whether a given action had those features, he could deduce whether or not it was a pious action. The difficulty arose in determining which were the defining characteristics. At first one might try to identify them as the characteristics common to a certain group of actions. But the very problem to begin with was that of deciding which actions were pious, and hence which to include in this group. Some actions may be clear cases of piety, but others are more doubtful and it was for the sake of them that a definition was required initially. Clearly, the set of common characteristics which can be extracted from a group of actions depends on the actions which make up the group; if the chosen sample contains only the clear cases then very likely there will be some extraneous and inessential features to be found among the common characteristics, and the resulting definition will rule out genuine cases which lack these superfluous features. But if this way of identifying the defining characteristics of piety is unavailable to us, we must find some other way or else we cannot even set out to discover which ones they are. Of course, we must first be able to determine whether any proposed method really does identify piety and not some other property, and I do not see how this will be possible unless at some point we simply stipulate concerning some method that the property we are looking for is whichever one it happens to identify. The sooner we make this stipulation the sooner we can answer the question 'What is piety?'; for, construed as a factual question and not as a practical question about what to do, nothing except the use of words ever depended on its solution anyway.

Consider for example the question 'What is a lie?'. If we try to answer this by considering only the obvious cases of lies we will find that they all share the property of being false statements made with the intent to deceive. But we may legitimately wonder whether to be a lie a statement must actually be false or need only be believed to be false by the liar. Sartre, in his play *Le Mur*, tells of a resistance fighter captured by the Gestapo who eventually tells the interrogators that his companions are hiding in a place where he is sure they are not. But his companions, fearful that he might reveal their true location, decide to move; as it happens, they relocate to the very place he mentioned to the Gestapo, and are consequently captured. Did he lie? We know that he intended to deceive his interrogators and that he unknowingly told them something true instead. We also know that his statement's being a lie, if it is one, consists in nothing more than these two features of it. So if we know whether it has these features how can we fail to know whether it is a lie? Again it seems that any doubt we might have about the matter does not concern what he actually did, but only what is the correct word for what he did. And this is a linguistic question, not a moral one. You may call it a 'conceptual' question if you wish, but glorifying it with that title does not alter the fact that it is answered either by consulting the dictionary to find out how other people use the relevant word, or simply by deciding how to use it in the future.

Now when Meno asked whether virtue could be taught, Socrates answered that he had no idea since he did not know what virtue was. Moreover, he claimed that he could not know anything at all about virtue until he found out what it was, and as an illustration he pointed out that he could not have known whether Meno was wealthy or good looking unless he had first known who Meno was. This provoked Meno to wonder how Socrates could so much as set out to enquire what virtue was if he had no idea what it was whose nature he was enquiring after. Even if he stumbled across it, how would he recognize it as the object of his search if he knew nothing at all about it that could serve as a mark of identification? Meno's challenge, of course, is a perfectly general one. It is difficult to see how can know whether a certain object has a given feature if we do not even know which object we are talking about; and it is just as difficult to see how we can ever find out which object it is unless we already know some identifying feature of it by which we can recognize it.

Let us pursue for a while the illustration which Socrates provided and ask how we would set about discovering whether Meno was wealthy. It seems obvious that in order to do this we must first find out who he was. And for our purposes it will be enough if we find some description which is true of Meno and of no one else. This will count as knowing who Meno was even if we do not know what he looked like and would be unable to recognize him in a police line-up. Suppose to begin with that all we know about Meno is that he was a young aristocrat who had occasion to discuss philosophy with Socrates. This description is one which applies equally to many different men, and although it tells us something about Meno it does not tell us enough about who he was to enable us to determine whether he was wealthy. Let us then suppose that for each of the youthful interlocutors of Socrates we have a description which distinguishes him from all the rest. One of them prosecuted his father for murder, another was a general who defected to Sparta, a third became one of the Thirty Tyrants, a fourth was put to death at Babylon, a fifth wrote dialogues, and so on. And imagine further that we know of each of them whether he was wealthy, but do not know which one was Meno. In that case we would know whether the one who died at Babylon was wealthy but not whether Meno was wealthy even though Meno was the one who died at Babylon.

But what do we learn by discovering whether Meno was wealthy that we don't already know once we have found out that the man who died at Babylon was wealthy, if they are the same person? Apparently we can know *of* a certain man, who happens to be Meno, whether he was wealthy without at the same time knowing whether Meno was wealthy. There must then be something we know about this man when we know he is Meno that we don't know when we know only that he is the interlocutor of Socrates who died at Babylon. Otherwise the statement that Meno was wealthy would tell us no more than the statement that the interlocutor of Socrates who died at

Babylon was wealthy; and then once we had established the truth of
the second statement it would not be a further question whether the
first was true.

If, for instance, to say that Meno was wealthy were just to attribute
wealth to a certain man then we would already have said this much if
we had said that the interlocutor who died at Babylon was wealthy –
even if we did not know that Meno died in Babylon. To say the latter
is to ascribe wealth (as well as death at Babylon) to a certain person,
and whether we know it or not this happens to be the same person we
ascribe it to when we say the former. So when we asserted the latter
we would be saying everything we say when we asserted the former,
and more besides. And from this it follows that if we knew the latter
we would know everything and more that the former tells us, since
what we know when we know something is the same as what we are
saying when we assert it. So if there is to be any point in wondering
whether the former is true once we have established the truth of the
latter it must be because we know something about a man when we
are told that he is Meno that we do not know when we are told only
that he is the interlocutor who died at Babylon. And the point will
then be to find out whether this extra bit of information, whatever it
is, also applies to someone who was wealthy.

And of course we do know something, namely that he was the
principal character other than Socrates in the dialogue named after
him. But suppose the question arose how we know that this character
was really Meno and that Plato was not representing someone else
under the same name as Meno's in order to protect that person's
identity. To ask this question would betray a misunderstanding of the
nature of the claim that he was the principal antagonist of the *Meno*.
Most of us are introduced to Meno through Plato's dialogue and not,
for example, through Xenophon's *Anabasis*. For us Meno is simply
whoever it happens to be that Plato was representing as talking with
Socrates in that dialogue; that is who *we* intend to be talking about
when we use the name 'Meno'. It is certainly an empirical assumption
that there ever was a person of that description and that the character
in the dialogue was not a fiction. It is also an empirical assumption
that this person, whoever he was, bore the name 'Meno' in real life,
and this assumption could be disconfirmed by finding independent
sources who relate a very similar conversation, universally alleged to
be unique, between Socrates and someone of a different name. In
other words, it is an empirical hypothesis that Meno ever existed and
was called 'Meno' by anyone except Plato. But it is not an empirical

hypothesis that Meno was the person Plato was characterizing in the *Meno*. If he is anyone at all, he is just whoever that person turns out to be.

Clearly there must be something we know about Meno that is not subject to empirical confirmation, for otherwise it would always make sense to ask whether it was Meno we were investigating or someone else. If the claim that Meno had a particular characteristic, F, were a testable hypothesis then there would have to be some way of identifying him (that is, of specifying who he was) other than as the possessor of that characteristic. But he can be identified at all only as the contingent possessor of some characteristics or other, and all that we can do to find out whether Meno had characteristic F is to discover, of some characteristic or other, whether their unique possessor also had F. Thus, if we are to investigate whether he had feature F there must be some other feature G he was known to possess uniquely so that we can procede by enquiring whether the person who had G also had F. If it is also open to empirical confirmation whether he had feature G then there must be some further characteristic H by which he can be identified independently of his possession of either F or G. But this cannot go on forever. It makes sense to question the attribution of some property to an individual only if there is a way of saying who he is or a criterion specifying his identity which is independent of his being the bearer of that property. So it cannot make sense to question every characterization of him because in the absence of any description immune from doubt there would no way of being sure who it was whose possession of these characteristics we were questioning.

If for *every* property we know to be a feature of Meno there must have been a further property we used to specify his identity in order to discover that he had the first property to begin with, so that we required a second specification even in order to determine that he fit the first one, then obviously we would have to know an infinite number of things about him before we knew anything at all. To stop this regress there must come a point where we are prepared to substitute some description or cluster of descriptions for the proper name in the question 'Was Meno wealthy?' and to stipulate that our question is about *whoever* should happen to satisfy that description, or satisfies a significant number of descriptions in the cluster, and about no one else. At this point it is no longer an empirical claim that Meno fits that specification. The stipulation does not have the result that a certain person magically acquires the properties mentioned in the description, but rather ensures that we are referring only to someone who does have those properties.[7]

Let us now imagine a dispute that could be pictorially represented as follows. Two people are preparing a list of all the companions of Socrates. On the left-hand side of the page there appears a column of definite descriptions: 'the interlocutor of Socrates who prosecuted his father for murder',' . . . who defected as a general to Sparta',' . . . who became one of the Thirty Tyrants', and so on. Opposite them on the right-hand side is the name 'Meno'; arrows with question-marks lead from the name to each of the descriptions. And at the head of the page is the question 'Was he wealthy?.' For each of the descriptions on the left-hand side the people preparing the list are in complete agreement about whether the man who satisfies it was wealthy. The only issue on which they disagree concerns whether Meno was wealthy. And this is because they do not agree about who Meno was, although they agree that he was one of the men described on the left-hand side. One of them says that Meno was the man who had feature F, and this man was wealthy. The other admits that the man who had feature F was indeed wealthy, but insists that Meno was the man who had feature G and that this man was not wealthy.

Now of course they cannot resolve this dispute by setting out to discover whether Meno was the man who had feature F or the man who had feature G unless they can agree upon a way of specifying his identity independently of his possessing either F or G and unless the specification is such that they can determine whether someone satisfies it. Sooner or later each of them must arrive at a way of identifying Meno that he does not regard as open to question, simply because he has run out of further specifications without which it can make no sense to go on asking whether Meno is really the man he is identified as being. At this point each will take the subject of their dispute to be simply whoever satisfies the description he has ended up with. But if they end up with different descriptions which fit different men, one of whom was wealthy and the other was not, then in virtue of what are they even talking about the same man? One of them tries to show the other that the man who satisfies description X was wealthy, and the other in turn tries to show that the man who satisfies description Y was not. And each succeeds in convincing the other, so that now there is nothing left for them to dispute. It cannot be a further question for them whether Meno was wealthy since they both agree that to know of a man that he is Meno is not to know anything about him that is not already contained in the information either that he satisfies description X or that he satisfies description Y. And it is nonsense to suppose that they can set about determining which description provides the 'correct' specification of Meno's identity, for unless they can describe in advance whose identity it is they are trying to specify, they can have no idea whether any specification they come up with identifies the man they are looking for or someone else.

When we attempt to identify characteristics and properties, the same considerations apply. Socrates said that he did not know whether virtue could be taught because he did not know what virtue was. Presumably virtue is a disposition to behave in a certain way. But so is vice. What Socrates claimed to lack was a way of identifying virtue and distinguishing it from other dispositions. He needed to know exactly what sort of behaviour virtue was a disposition to engage in before he could determine whether it was possible, by teaching, to inculcate into someone a disposition to behave in precisely that way.

Now imagine people engaged in a dispute that could be diagrammed in a way similar to that about the identity of Meno. On the left-hand side of the page are listed dispositions to engage in various empirically described behaviour; on the right-hand side is the word 'virtue' and arrows with question-marks lead from it to each of the characterizations on the left. At the top of the page is the question 'Can it be taught?' With regard to each of the dispositions listed on the left everyone is in agreement about whether it can be taught. They disagree only about whether virtue can be taught, and this is because they do not agree about which of the dispositions it is, though they all agree it is one of them. If, as we have been supposing for the sake of argument, it is a fact about someone that he is virtuous, and his being virtuous is the same as his having one of these dispositions, e.g. one which can be called 'disposition D', then how is it possible to know whether disposition D can be taught without at the same time knowing whether virtue can be taught? This can only happen if thinking of the disposition as being identical with virtue is different from thinking of it as disposition D. This turn requires that the notion of virtue contain concepts which are not contained in the notion of disposition D.

In order to discover which of the empirically characterized dispositions on the list is identical with virtue, we must be able to come up with a way of identifying virtue that is independent of any of the characterizations comprising the list. And if it is still an empirical

matter whether the specification we come up with really identifies
virtue, then the question whether it does will always be what Moore
called an 'open question' rather than a self-answering question like
'Is virtue identical with virtue?'. But if it is a genuine question then
we must have yet a further specification of virtue which is independent of the first one. And if this is not to go on forever, we must
eventually arrive at a specification about which it is not an empirical
matter whether it actually succeeds in picking out virtue rather than
some other disposition.

   If at this point there is still disagreement about which is the correct
specification then I do not see how it can amount to anything more
than a verbal dispute. For supposedly the parties to the dispute have
reached the point where their notions of virtue are *identical* with the
notions involved in the specifications they use to identify it. Although
they may think they are talking about the same characteristic or
disposition, this is impossible if they are at the stage where they use
the same word synonymously with two different specifications describing two different characteristics. At the beginning they could
suppose themselves to be engaged in a genuine dispute of an empirical nature, since even if the sense of the word 'virtue' were different
from the sense of the specification 'disposition D' the two expressions
might still have the same reference. The senses of these expressions
embody different ways of identifying what they refer to; and it is an
empirical matter whether they are ways of identifying the same thing.
But if it turns out that they are unable to agree even about which
sense or route of identification is attached to the word 'virtue' then
they are lost. For they cannot sensibly discuss whether two routes of
identification lead to the same thing if they cannot even agree on
which routes they are talking about.

   The question must now move to the linguistic plane. Since they
evidently associate two different concepts with the same word, there
is nothing left to discuss except perhaps the question which of these
concepts is generally attached to the word by competent speakers of
the language. But why was the answer to this question ever thought
to have any philosophical relevance? Why is it important to find out
whether people in general or I in particular use the word 'virtue' to
mean one thing rather than another? There are many different ways
in which we might in fact be using the word, and therefore many
different judgements which sentences containing it might express. If
we are not sure in which of these ways we actually do employ it, or
have employed it in the past, then we ought simply to decide which

judgements we want to express with it, and then make sure that our audiences know which of the many possible uses we have in fact adopted. It does not matter in the least which use this is, since the choice is a linguistic one and not a moral one. It is a choice of meanings and is nothing to be resisted since no one changes his mind or alters his beliefs by attaching a different meaning to the words he uses, any more than when he speaks a different language. He merely uses different words to express the same beliefs, attitudes, and intentions he has always held.

   The only conceivable ground for preferring to assign one meaning rather than another is that doing so will preserve the sense with which the word is generally used at present. But it is precisely what this sense is that is so difficult to determine since people's linguistic intuitions are not sufficiently clear or uniform and are in just as much conflict as their moral intuitions. One way of trying to find out which concept we express by a word, or what we mean by it, is to ask what we would say in various hypothetical circumstances, or how we would describe them. But if we are not sure what we would say of certain situations, or if we would not all say the same thing, then we will not get very far with this method.

STATEMENTS OF FACT AND DESCRIPTIVE PREDICATES

Let us return to the utilitarian and deontologist disputing whether it would be wrong to punish an innocent person in order to prevent greater suffering to other innocent people. Now one consequence of the view that they are disputing a factual question about what is true or false rather than a practical issue about what to do, is that their moral intuitions are nothing but linguistic intuitions. For suppose that we are simply stating a fact about the punishment when we call it right or wrong. What exactly is it to state a fact? I think a proper explanation would proceed by first saying what it is to state an 'atomic' fact and then go on to explain in terms of this other kinds of factual statements such as conjunctions, hypotheticals, negations, as well as universal and existential propositions. In order to state an atomic fact you must first of all refer to an object and ascribe some feature to it. When the object referred to has the feature ascribed to it, the statement is said to be true and the object is said to satisfy the predicate used to ascribe this feature. Secondly, the predicate must be of the sort whose sense determines its extension, i.e. the class of things to which it applies. This is what R. M. Hare calls a 'descriptive predicate': it is one whose sense lays down the conditions a thing must meet to satisfy it.[8]

For instance, the sentence 'This stone is magnetic' is used to state a fact only if the referent of the expression 'this stone' satisfies the descriptive predicate 'is magnetic'; and this predicate is a descriptive one only if it has the extension it does because of its sense. To know its sense is to know what sorts of things satisfy it, or at least to know what you must find out to discover what satisfies it. It is to know which external properties (e.g. attracting iron filings, affecting compass needles) are such that in order to fall within the predicate's extension a thing must have whatever hidden constitution is in fact responsible for producing those properties. Knowing the sense does not tell you which constitution this is, but it gives you an identifying description of it (namely 'the constitution responsible for producing these observable characteristics').

On the other hand, the sentence 'This stone is to be avoided' is not used to state a fact because even if the stone is to be avoided, and can thus be said to satisfy the predicate 'is to be avoided', nevertheless the predicate is not a descriptive one since its sense does not determine when something satisfies it. One can be told what it *means* to say that something is to be avoided without thereby being told what sorts of things *are* to be avoided. Of course, the sense of the predicate 'is to be avoided' lays it down that in order to be included within its extension an object must be something to stay away from. But this only tells you what it is to avoid something; it does not tell you what to avoid.

Furthermore, I use sentences of the form 'X is to be avoided by Y' as simply the result of putting into the passive voice sentences of the form 'Y is to avoid X'. And when I tell someone that he is to avoid a thing, I am merely telling him to avoid it, which is to issue a prescription of some sort and not to state a fact.

Suppose that the words 'right' and 'wrong' were descriptive predicates, so that we could know what sorts of things satisfied them merely by knowing their sense. To determine what their sense is, we have only to notice what sorts of things we *think* satisfy them; we observe what we would say of certain states of affairs, or whether we would use those predicates to characterize them. And this is just to observe our linguistic intuitions. It will of course require empirical investigation to find out what sort of thing a given object really is, but there will come a point where only linguistic intuitions are required to determine whether anything of that sort falls within the extension of a given predicate. Now if our utilitarian and deontologist agree on every fact about the punishment except whether it would be wrong, then they must identify the wrongness of an action with different empirical features. Again, this could amount to a genuine difference of opinion only if they attached the same empirical concept to the word 'wrong' but disagreed about which *other* empirical concepts were coextensive with it. But ex hypothesi they have arrived at the point where each holds that the concept he claims to be coextensive with the one he attaches to the word 'wrong' is not another concept at all but identical with it, so that all he *means* by calling an action wrong is that it has this empirical feature. However, they both agree about whether the proposed punishment has this feature, and only appear to disagree because they attach different concepts to the same word. All that is left for them to dispute is the question which concept is attached to the word by the majority of competent speakers. And there is nothing of philosophical or moral importance whatever to be revealed by finding out how people actually use the words 'right' and 'wrong' once we agree on all the facts which we could ever decide to use those words to state.

DOING WITHOUT A DEFINITION OF MORALITY

The dilemma I have been at pains to construct is this. If wrongness is a non-empirical property of actions then we ought to be able to test such claims as that all punishment of the innocent is wrong by detecting an act's wrongness independently of knowing any empirical fact about it, such as whether it is a case of punishment at all. But obviously this cannot be done. Or if wrongness is an empirical feature then people who agree on all the empirical facts about an action but disagree about its moral status can only be engaged in a verbal dispute; they use the same word to ascribe different features.

What we require, then, is an explanation of how two people could *mean* the same thing by calling an action wrong if they did not ultimately agree on what it was for an action to *be* wrong. There is an explanation, but it is one according to which the word 'wrong' is not descriptive predicate. In that case no one could misuse the term by including in its extension something which is excluded by the sense of the expression, because it would not be the sort of word whose sense determined the conditions a thing must meet to satisfy it. And this

would be the case if the moral judgement that it would be wrong to
punish the prisoner logically entailed a negative answer to the practical question whether or not to punish him; for two people can mean
the same thing by asking what is to be done (with regard to the
punishment) without ever agreeing about what is to be done, since
knowing what it *means* to say that something is to be done does not
tell you what sorts of things *are* to be done.

Now it is entirely a linguistic matter whether we actually use the
word 'wrong' so that sentences of the form 'X is wrong' express
judgements which follow logically from statements of fact or whether
they express judgements which entail prescriptions to action and are
neither true nor false. We shall see later (in Chapter 2) why, except in
a few uninteresting circumstances, they cannot do both. But in order
to realize that nothing of any substance depends on this semantical
question, observe what happens when a deontologist attempts to
convince a utilitarian not to punish the prisoner. The utilitarian asks
'Why not punish him?.' If he is told simply that it would be wrong to
do so, then there are a number of moves open to him depending on
whether he takes the wrongness of an action to be a sufficient reason
not to do it. Suppose that in fact he does, i.e. he assents to the
prescription 'If an action is wrong then don't do it.' Now one of the
few things we know about what it means to call an action wrong is
that actions are wrong in virtue of some feature they possess. The
utilitarian will therefore ask 'Why is it wrong?' or 'What feature of
the punishment makes it wrong?.' And the answer will be that the
prisoner is innocent.

He is thus faced with the following argument:

(1) If the prisoner is innocent then it is wrong to punish him.
(2) If it is wrong to punish him then don't punish him.

∴ (3) If the prisoner is innocent then don't punish him.

Having accepted premise (2) he can avoid the conclusion only by
denying premise (1), that the prisoner's innocence makes it wrong to
punish him. And as a utilitarian this is precisely the step he will take if
he believes that more harm will result in the short- and long-run by not
making an example of him. The utilitarian who does not see the
prisoner's innocence as a sufficient reason *not to punish* him will
certainly not see it as a sufficient reason why it would be *wrong to
punish* him, if he is being consistent and already thinks the wrongness

of an act is a conclusive reason not to do it. On the other hand, if he accepted premise (1) he would have to deny premise (2) if he still wished to avoid being logically committed to the conclusion. In that case he would not see the wrongness of the punishment as a sufficient reason not to impose it if he did not already see the prisoner's innocence as such a reason.

In any case, determining whether his innocence makes it wrong to punish the prisoner is no help whatever in answering the question 'Why not punish him?.' For either his innocence is a sufficient reason by itself not to punish him or it isn't. If it is, then it doesn't matter whether it also makes it wrong to punish him or whether its being wrong is itself a sufficient reason to do it. On the other hand, if his innocence is not a sufficient reason not to punish him, then it still doesn't matter since in that case either his innocence doesn't make it wrong or its being wrong isn't a sufficient reason not to do it; for of three propositions P, Q, and R, if P does not not entail R then Q cannot both entail R and also follow from P.

It is a waste of time to answer the question 'Why not do X?' by saying that it would be wrong to do it, because this only invites the question 'Why is it wrong?.' And since it is precisely the same answer which is given to both questions, we might as well have dispensed with the moral claim and gone straight to the answer that had to be given anyway, either sooner or later. It is exactly as if that Indian philosopher made so famous by Locke had explained how the Earth sat suspended in mid-air by claiming that it rested on the back of a giant elephant, and when asked how the elephant was suspended immediately launched into an exposition of Newton's Laws of Motion. There is no point in his hesitating to give the real reason until after he has mentioned the elephant because the very question which the elephant was used to answer has to arise with regard even to it, and whatever eventually explains the elephant will explain the Earth without the elephant. Now it is the same answer that is given to both the practical question 'Why not punish the prisoner?' and the moral question 'Why would it be wrong to punish him?', namely '. . . because he is innocent'. And if it is an adequate answer to the moral question, then in order for that to be relevant it would have to be an adequate answer to the practical question as well, even without inserting the moral claim; for if it were a sufficient answer to the moral question but not to the practical one then not even the moral claim would be a sufficient answer to the practical question. If P entails Q, but does not entail R, then Q does not entail R either. So just as in the case of the elephant, to insert the moral pronouncement between the practical question and the eventual answer to it is simply to stall for time.[9]

Those who still think that moral questions are important will no doubt object that a consideration could provide sufficient reason not to do something without making it wrong to do it; it may indeed be wrong, but not for that reason. A gaoler might be offered a substantial bribe not to serve his prisoners spoiled food, and the size of the bribe might be sufficient reason to do this. But there is another sufficient reason, which is the fact that spoiled food will make the prisoners sick, and surely it is this fact rather than the size of the bribe that makes it wrong. The size of the bribe just makes it foolish. And it will be claimed that if we distinguish from among the sufficient reasons to do or not to do something those which make it morally obligatory or morally wrong to do it, then people can be said to act from moral reasons rather than, for example, out of self-interest or expedience if the reasons that persuade them either to do or not to do a particular thing are also the reasons why it would be morally right or wrong to do it. Consequently it is thought that in addition to the question whether or not to do something, and why, we ought also to ask whether it would be right or wrong to do it, and why. For if we know what makes actions right or wrong we can determine whether the reasons that persuaded a person to act in the way he did were moral or non-moral reasons.

But why do we want to determine this? What question depends for its answer on deciding whether some consideration is a moral or a non-moral reason? We have indeed an absorbing interest in the practical question: which kinds of considerations to encourage people to act from: parents in particular have to decide which sorts of reasons they shall bring up their children to treat as overriding. It matters to us very much which sorts of reasons will motivate people to do various things under different circumstances. But it does not matter at all, except for purposes of communication, which sort of reason is to fall within the extension of the term 'moral'.

Suppose we have committed ourselves to letting moral considerations override all others, which means that we have decided to do what there are moral reasons to do even when there are reasons of another sort not to do it. If our commitment has led us into a dispute about whether a given fact does or does not provide a moral reason for doing something then it is difficult to see how our dispute could have any point unless it were really a disguised disagreement about whether *to let* that reason override or be overridden by others, which is a practical matter of what to do and not a factual matter of what is true or false. For if it were a fact about a consideration whether it was a moral reason or not, and we disagreed about what it was for something to be a moral reason, then our only recourse would be to examine what we are *saying* about it when we *call* it a moral reason. It is an obvious fact, though a contingent one, that we use the expression 'moral reason' to call something a moral reason; we might have used some other expression or spoken a different language. But given this fact, we can find out what a moral reason is by discovering which properties we happen to use this expression to ascribe to things, which of course is determined by the sense we attach to the expression (supposing that it is a descriptive predicate). But now we have left morals far behind and are firmly ensconced in semantics. We ought not to waste our time attempting to determine what we actually do mean by this predicate and instead simply decide what we shall mean. Nothing at all hinges on this decision, for if we make it a descriptive predicate then it will have to be a further (practical) question whether to let considerations that satisfy this predicate override others; and if instead we make it a condition that in order to satisfy it a consideration must be one that is to override other sorts, then the predicate will not be a descriptive one and the question whether something is a moral reason will not be a factual one.

For instance, suppose I say 'Let this sort of consideration override all others', and you ask 'Why?'. If I reply '. . . because considerations of that sort are moral ones' then obviously we are right back with the elephant. For if you already intend to treat moral considerations as overriding, your next question will be: 'But what is it about such considerations that makes them moral ones?.' And the answer I give to this will be the same as the one I should have given to your original question if I had not been stalling. I will maintain that they are moral reasons by virtue of having certain features; if you agree that they have these features but deny that having them is sufficient to make them moral reasons then it seems that the only way for our disagreement to be something more than a verbal dispute about what is *meant* by calling something a moral reason is for it to be a disagreement about a practical and not a theoretical matter, namely, about which features are such that considerations having them are to override all others.

On the other hand, if it were a theoretical matter and we could determine which were the moral reasons independently of deciding which sorts of reasons to act on in case of a conflict, then it would be foolish to commit oneself to letting moral reasons override all others before determining which the moral reasons were. It would be like resolving to believe whatever it should happen to say in the Bible without first bothering to find out what the Bible actually said. And if a dispute breaks out over which features, of all those agreed to characterize a given reason, make it either a moral or a non-moral reason then again we must wonder how such a dispute could be anything but verbal. The utilitarian and deontologist, for example, will agree that pointing out how much suffering will be prevented by the punishment is to appeal to the consequences of the act; it is to advance forward-looking considerations. They will also agree that pointing out the prisoner's innocence is to appeal to what the prisoner has or hasn't done, and is therefore to advance backward-looking considerations. So they agree on which are the forward-looking and which are the backward-looking reasons; they disagree only about which are the moral reasons. And they cannot even say what difference it makes whether something is a moral reason or not.

THE SUBJECT MATTER OF A SOCRATIC DIALOGUE

Socrates spent a good deal of time talking about such things as virtue, courage, justice, piety, friendship, and beauty. He wanted to know what they were. What are we to make of this? In the considered opinion of most analytic philosophers, an opinion which affects even their translations, he was engaged in a sort of semantical exercise. Thus we have the remark of a famous logician:

> Socrates was the first to enquire into the ethical virtues asking "What is piety?" and "What is the just?", and thought that by answering such questions he would be able to perceive the "essence" of those virtues. What he really did was to solve the problem "What is meant, in Greek of course, by the words 'piety' or 'the just'?", and he tried to determine their meaning by inductive arguments in form of definitions. (Jan Lukasiewicz, The Principle of Individuation', Symposium, *Aristotelian Society Supp.* vol. 27, 1953, p. 150)

According to this view he was trying to pin down the exact meaning of certain Greek words. It is also said that he was undertaking a conceptual enquiry by investigating the concept of justice or courage, and that he was more interested in what the concepts were themselves than in the fact that particular Greek words were used to express them. But it all amounts to the same thing since our point of departure and basic clue in the search for these concepts is the contingent linguistic fact that certain words are used to express them. We identify them initially as simply whichever concepts competent speakers of the language happen to use these words to express. To discover which concepts they are we have to observe the relevant ways in which people actually use the words, noting in particular which hypothetical situations they would use them to describe.

But there is no guarantee at all that linguistic intuitions will remain uniform when the contemplated situations are far removed from common experience, and then we are reduced to counting how many would say one thing, how many would say something else, and how many are undecided. Some people are convinced, for instance, that they use the words 'right' and 'wrong' as descriptive predicates; others are equally convinced that they do not. What is the point of arguing about it? If there are different ways in which we might be using these words then the sensible thing is not to enquire how the majority uses them but rather to decide on a use and make sure our audience knows which it is.

If Socrates was not investigating the meanings of words, then what was he doing? Perhaps he did not know exactly, since different sorts of enquiry had not then been clearly distinguished. A more promising question to ask is 'How might *we* profitable read Socratic dialogues otherwise than as linguistic investigations?.' And my recommendation is that they be read as dealing with practical issues about what to do and how to live rather than with theoretical questions about what is true or false. To illustrate this distinction, let us take as an example the word 'wrong' and suppose that sentences of the form 'X is wrong' mean simply 'Don't anyone ever do X.'[10] It is irrelevant whether this correctly characterizes the meaning of 'wrong'; that is a linguistic question. All that concerns us at the moment is what follows from the supposition that it does. If it does then we can distinguish two different questions about the word which would otherwise have the same answer, namely 'What is the meaning or sense of the word?' and 'What is the criterion of its correct application?.' If 'wrong' were a descriptive predicate then its sense would determine the sort of thing to which it was correctly applied. But on our supposition it is not a descriptive predicate. The sense of the word tells you only that to call an action wrong is to say that no one is ever to do it, which is just to forbid the action universally. This is part of the *meaning* of the word since anyone who heard me say 'Don't anyone ever do this' and didn't realize that I was forbidding people to do something would not have understood what I said. The sense of the word does not determine in addition which sorts of actions are not to be done, or which actions it is 'correct' to forbid. It does indeed tell you that the actions to be forbidden are the ones which are to be prohibited, but again this only tells you what it is to forbid an action, not which actions to forbid. So according to our supposition, knowing what it is that we are saying about an action when we call it wrong does not tell us which sorts of actions are correctly *called* wrong, or hence which actions really *are* wrong. Something else is required for that. At least part of deciding which actions are 'wrong' in this sense is deciding which things never to do.

Now we know from the meaning of the word 'piety' that it has to do with respect rendered towards the gods and our parents. If it were a descriptive expression then we could find out exactly what sort of respectful behaviour piety consisted in by looking to the sense of the word. But when we already know the different sorts of respectful behaviour there are, what difference does it make whether the word is used by most competent speakers to denote one kind rather than another? After all, finding out how people use a word is of no help whatever in answering the question I think was of most interest to Socrates in this matter, namely how to behave toward gods and parents, or what sort of respect to show them.

Courage is the virtue whose sphere of exercise comprises those occasions when we are faced with danger or sacrifice. Someone who wanted to know exactly which behavioural disposition was identical with courage might think that he could find out by using as a premise the contingent proposition that the word 'courage' is used to denote it. But the only thing it is possible to learn by linguistic analysis is which disposition is commonly denoted by the word. And the fact that one disposition rather than another enjoys this distinction is certainly no reason to acquire it for oneself or inculcate it into anyone else. However, aside from the semantical question, there are important practical issues to consider such as which sorts of danger to face and which to back down from, which sorts of risk to take for the sake of what kind of prize and at what chances of success.

These were the issues about which Socrates was most concerned, and, according to my perhaps contentious translation, he said so:

'The most noble of all enquiries, Callicles, is the one concerning those things about which you have just censured me, namely what sort of man one is to be, and what to occupy oneself with, and to what extent when one is both old and young' (*Gorgias*, 487 e7–488 a2). 'And do not thus accept what I say as though I were playing; for you see that this is what our discussion is about – and what would a man of even small intelligence take more seriously than this – namely how one is to live' (ibid., 500 cl–4).

2   Some Aspects of the Logic of Prescriptions

We constantly find ourselves wondering what to do. We are placed in circumstances where a decision between alternative courses of action is required of us, and we ask either individually 'What shall I do?' or collectively 'What shall we do?.' Before we finally accept an answer to either of these questions we may wish to acquaint ourselves with certain facts, such as the likely consequences of each of the proposed alternatives or their compatibility with other things we may wish to do. But having ascertained the facts to the best of our ability we must again face up to the question what to do. It will not go away simply because we have addressed ourselves to questions of fact instead. The only way of answering the question 'What shall I do?' is by *deciding* what to do; and though adopting a certain view of the facts may influence the decision we make, we shall see that it cannot logically commit us to making one decision rather than another, except in rather peculiar and uninteresting circumstances.

UNIVERSAL AND PAST-TENSE PRESCRIPTIONS

When we ask someone what to do, he may answer us in one of a variety of ways. Depending on the situation he may urge, request, order or tell us to do something; or he might advise, suggest or recommend that we do it. There are no doubt many other ways of answering our question, but in spite of their diversity they seem to have something in common which makes them all ways of answering it. Not all answers take the form of telling us to do something; when we are seeking advice on what to do, we do not usually appreciate someone telling us what to do or ordering us about. Remember the famous fatherly counsel of Polonius: 'And these few precepts in thy memory: Look thou character. Give thy thoughts no tongue, Nor any unproportioned thought his act. Be thou familiar, but by no means vulgar: . . . Give every man thy ear, but few thy voice, Take each man's censure, but reserve thy judgement. . . . Neither a borrower nor a lender be, . . . This above all: to thine own self be true, . . .' (*Hamlet*, I, iii, 58–80). All this is given in the imperative mood; yet it is offered as advice and not as a list of orders. On the other hand, a commanding officer is supposed to give his subordinates commands rather than suggestions. What I wish to say about these different types of answers to the question 'What shall I do?', all given in the imperative mood, is that they are species of 'prescriptions'; they are different ways of 'prescribing' an action. But what exactly is a prescription? What is this common feature to which I have merely attached a name? Professor Hare has attempted to define it in terms of the conditions for sincere assent to prescriptions. Using the term 'command' as a blanket expression covering all the kinds of utterances I have called prescriptions, he writes:

> If we assent to a statement we are said to be sincere in our assent if and only if we believe that it is true (believe what the speaker has said). If, on the other hand, we assent to a second-person command addressed to ourselves, we are said to be sincere in our assent if and only if we do or resolve to do what the speaker has told us to do; if we do not do it but only resolve to do it later, then if, when the occasion arises for doing it, we do not do it, we are said to have changed our mind; we are no longer sticking to the assent which we previously expressed. (*The Language of Morals*, OUP, 1952, pp. 19–20)

This does very nicely for prescriptions addressed to ourselves. For instance, we cannot correctly be said to accept someone's advice if we do not intend to follow it and do what he advises; and if I agree to do what someone requests of me, my agreement cannot be sincere if I have no intention of doing what he requests.

This definition can be extended to certain prescriptions addressed by ourselves to others. If I make a statement of fact, thereby telling someone that something is the case, my statement or assertion is sincere if and only if I believe that what I have told him is true. And, following Hare's definition, when I prescribe that someone do something my prescription is sincere if and only if I intend that he do what I prescribe. But what is it to intend that another person or an inanimate object should do something? If I am playing golf and slice the ball into the trees, I might naturally say that I didn't intend the ball to land in the rough, I intended it to land on the green. But surely this can only mean that I intended *to do something* which in the circumstances would result in the ball landing on the green. In this case my intention was unfulfilled because my action did not have the intended result. Now on the strength of this single paradigm I shall risk advancing the following generalization: to intend that some event occur is to intend to do something which in the circumstances will result in that event occuring (unless the event is a 'basic action', such as raising one's arm usually is, for which there is no other action we perform in order to bring it about).

I may, for instance, intend that someone pass me the salt by virtue of intending to ask someone to pass it to me, believing that my request will result in the salt being passed to me. It must not be thought, however, that intention to get certain results by uttering that request is the same as the intention that determines what I meant by the utterance. As Hare once pointed out,

> it is not true of commands in general that the person who issues them is, *ex vi termini* trying to get people to do the things specified. The sadistic schoolmaster, who commands his boys to keep silent in the hope that this will cause them to talk so that he can beat them, is still commanding or telling them to keep quiet. ('Wanting: Some Pitfalls' in *Practical Inferences*, Macmillan, 1971, pp. 53–4)

If we are dealing with people who are counter-suggestible we would ask them to do one thing intending thereby that they do something else, in which case our request is of course insincere.

Trouble arises, however, when we attempt to apply this definition to what Hare calls 'universal prescriptions'. To say that it is morally wrong to commit suicide is, according to Hare, to prescribe universally that *no one* at *any* time (past, present, or future) commit suicide. To prescribe this sincerely is to *intend* that no one in the past, present or future commit suicide. But it is logically inconsistent to intend that no one ever have committed suicide when you know perfectly well that people already have. I have argued elsewhere[1] that universal prescriptions are incoherent because sincere assent to them entails having intentions which no one could ever have. Although universal prescriptions are specifically designed so that 'we can derive from them imperative sentences in all the persons, as well as in all the tenses' (*The Language of Morals*, p. 188) Hare acknowledges that there is something odd in the notion of a past tensed prescription:

It is obvious why we never command things to happen in the past; and therefore it might be said that a past imperative would be meaningless. I am not concerend to deny this – for in a sense an expression *is* meaningless if it could have no possible use; but nevertheless it will be seen that these sentences do have a function in my analysis, and therefore I must ask the reader to put up with them. There is perhaps an analogy with the use of imaginary numbers in mathematics (Ibid., pp. 53–4)

The last sentence in the above quotation has recently been given further elaboration:

My analogy with imaginary numbers in mathematics (*LM* p. 188) was intended to suggest that the uses permitted by ordinary language are extensible for technical purposes in the way that I am proposing. We learnt the use of the number-words in counting; and we cannot use the square root of minus one and its multiples in counting; yet mathematicians and physicists have found a use for it in their theories. We should not be put off, by the fact that past-tense imperatives do not by themselves have a use in commanding, from adopting an analysis of value-judgements which produces them as a by-product. ('Universal and Past-Tense Prescriptions: a Reply . . .', *Analysis*, vol. 39, no. 4, 1979, p. 164)

I agree that *if* imaginary numbers are innocent then so are past prescriptions. Yet I am perhaps naive enough to persist in distrusting any physical theory that employs imaginary numbers. There are, of course, harmless interpretations of imaginary number talk with which I have no quarrel. Let the symbol 'v' represent a vector of a certain magnitude pointing in a certain direction; then let 'jv' represent the vector which results when v is rotated counter-clockwise through 90 degrees; then, by iteration, the expression 'jjv' or equivalently 'j^2v' represents the result of rotating this vector through a further 90 degrees; but the vector which results from rotating v through 180 degrees is denoted by the expression '$-v$'; hence, $j^2v = -v$. But we must not conclude from this that $j^2 = -1$; for the symbol 'j' is used here as an operator and does not denote any number at all. To say that j is not a real number is simply to say that it is not really a number.

Problems in mechanics which concern objects oscillating back and forth along a straight line are often more conveniently analysed as

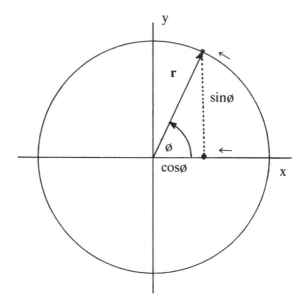

though the object's position were determined by the shadow cast by an imaginary object travelling in a circle about the line on which the oscillation actually occurs. If we take the centre of this circle to be the origin of a rectangular coordinate system then any point on the circle can be specified by its x- and y-coordinates, which are $\cos\phi$ and $\sin\phi$ respectively (if the radius of the circle = 1). We can thus represent any point on this circle by a vector **r** which begins at the origin and ends at the point; **r** is equal to the vector sum denoted by the expression '$\cos\phi + j\sin\phi$'. This is an instruction to proceed from the origin along the positive x- axis a distance of $\cos\phi$ units, then rotate counter-clockwise through 90 degrees and proceed in the direction of the positive y-axis a distance of $\sin\phi$ units. Now when we have finished with the mathematical analysis of the problem in terms of this circular motion, we then collect all the terms in the solution that contain 'j' and set them aside as representing that part of the motion that is purely *imaginary* in the literal sense; the rest of the terms in the solution describe the *real* part of the motion which takes place only along the x-axis.[2]

   This is just one important use which mathematicians and physicists have for the symbol 'j'. But does not require them to interpret j as any kind of number, imaginary or otherwise. The notion that there is a *number* whose square equals -1 is a notion which I confess I still find incoherent. Suppose I were to tell you that there is a number which added to itself equals 9, and which multiplied by itself also equals 9; well, $3 \times 3 = 9$ but $3 + 3 = 6$; and $4.5 + 4.5 = 9$ but 4.5×4.5 equals 20.25. If I were then to say 'but it is not a *real* number, it is just an *imaginary* number' you would quite reasonably conclude that there was *really* no such number at all. We might define a 'squound' to be a plane figure of 4 equals sides and 4 equal angles, all of whose points were equidistant from its centre. Suppose you say: 'But there is no such figure; only a circle has all its points equidistant from the centre, and it doesn't have 4 equal sides.' If I then reply 'Of course, it is not a real figure; it is just an imaginary one' you would properly interpret me as saying just that there is really no such figure as a squound.

As long as 'j' is interpreted as an operator or as a matrix there is nothing objectionable in its use, since operators and matrices are not numbers. But if it is used to represent an imaginary *number* then it is objectionable. And so are past *prescriptions* if these are defined in terms of conditions for sincere assent which require us to have impossible intentions. Now in fact the only prescriptions which Professor Hare defined in terms of assent conditions were second-person prescription addressed to ourselves; and I have tried to show what happens when other sorts of prescriptions are defined similarly. Perhaps there are other ways of defining them. In his article 'Relevance'[3] Hare writes: 'If a person is sincerely prescribing something, he *wants* it to happen' (p. 78). And this looks like an attempt to explain sincere prescription in terms of wanting. But in 'Wanting: Some Pitfalls' he sets out to explain wanting in terms of sincere prescription, following the suggestion of Geach and Kenny that 'to have a desire is to say-in-one's-heart an imperative' (p. 46). The relation between wanting something and intending to do something to get it is not very straightforward. A person might hope, and therefore wish, that someone resist a certain temptation and yet not wish to do anything to bring this about – he wants that person to resist all on his own.

The view expressed in 'Wanting: Some Pitfalls' are to a certain extent a modification of those I quoted from *The Language of Morals* and to that extent really dissolve the problem of past prescriptions. In *LM* it was said that we need universal prescriptions so that 'we can derive from them imperative sentences in all the persons, as well as in all the tenses' (p. 188). This is what gives us past imperatives. But in 'Wanting: Some Pitfalls' he writes as follows:

I may remark in passing that, if we do express wishes in words, this enables us to distinguish between two sorts of wishes which do need distinguishing, namely those which are naturally expressed in the imperative, and those which are naturally expressed in various 'optative' constructions (e.g. 'Would that I were a bird!'). This supports Miss Anscombe's distinction[4] between the kind of wanting of which 'the primitive sign is trying to get', and 'idle wishing'. We might say that the latter is idle, unlike the former, because its expression, unlike an imperative, does not command any action. (p. 51)

If sincerely to assent to the prescription that no one at any time ever commit suicide is to wish that no one ever do this, then part of the wish will be 'idle'. Instead of the past imperative sentence 'Do not have committed suicide', we will have the optative sentence 'Would that you had not committed suicide.' Since the latter does not prescribe any action there is no problem about intending to satisfy such a prescription. How much of the wish is not idle and involves intentions is a question that remains to be answered. For instance, I might intend *myself* never to commit suicide but I certainly don't intend to do anything to bring it about that no one in unborn, future generations ever commits suicide. The most, I think, that Hare can reasonably require is that from moral judgements we should be able to derive imperative sentences in *some* of the persons and *some* of the tenses, and optative sentences in the rest. Otherwise no one could sincerely assent to any moral judgement.

FUTURE PRESCRIPTIONS AND PAST VIOLATIONS

One consideration which tempts Hare to accept past tense prescriptions is the following. How, he asks, could a past action ever be a breach of a prescription we can issue in the present if the prescription did not forbid the occurence of the action in the past? And how could it forbid such an occurence unless it either is or entails a prescription in the past tense? Thus in teaching a person how to drive we might have occasion to say 'You ought to have let the clutch in more gently', and in saying this we would be trying to teach him the principle 'One ought to let the clutch in gently.' Elaborating on this, he says:

in such cases, instead of saying that we were teaching him how he *ought to* drive, we could almost equivalently say that we were teaching him how *to* drive, and in particular how *to* treat the clutch; the principle that we were teaching could, indeed, be expressed in the imperative: 'Always let the clutch in gently.' (Universal and Past-Tense Prescriptions: a Reply . . . ', p. 162).

The question then arises whether in this context 'always' means 'at all times; past, present, and future' or rather just 'from now on.' His argument that 'always' refers to past times, as well as future, is this:

> If I am to use a past breach of this principle in order to give instruction in the principle, it certainly looks as if the learner, when he let in the clutch too roughly, was breaking the *same* principle which I am still, now, trying to teach, him . . . and in teaching it we are clearly allowed by ordinary usage to point to past breaches in order to make clear to the learner exactly what the principle requires him to do or avoid. (Ibid., p. 162)

But it does not seem at all necessary, in order for a past action to be an *instance* of the sort of thing forbidden by a principle, that the principle entail past prescriptions so that the past action can also be a *breach* of it. We can say 'From now on, don't do what you just did, namely let the clutch in so roughly.' The learner is being told not to do in the future the *same* sort of thing he did in the past, and therefore his past action can be used to teach him what sort of thing he is not to do. His action was an instance of the sort of thing forbidden by this prescription, but it was not a breach of it because it occurred before the prescription was issued.

A different problem is the following: if we say prescriptively 'You should *have* let the clutch in more gently' we appear to be prescribing that he *have* let the clutch in more gently, which would be prescribing that something happen in the past. We cannot interpret this as saying merely 'You should let the clutch in more gently than you *did*' which is to prescribe for the future that he not do what he did in the past; for it is entirely possible that what he should do now is different from what he should have done previously. A music teacher does not contradict himself if he says to his pupil 'When you repeat this passage you should *now* play it more softly than you did, although to begin with you should *have* played it more loudly than you did.' To say that he should now perform differently than he did is not to imply that he should then have performed differently than he did.

One might try to solve this difficulty by supposing that 'You should have played that more loudly' expresses an "idle wish" and corresponds to the optative sentence 'Would that you had played that more loudly', whereas 'You should now play that more softly' expresses an intention and corresponds to the imperative sentence 'Now play that more softly.' But this solution presents two further problems of its own. First, it requires either that 'should have' and 'should now' be logically unanalysable and contain no common component, or else that the 'should' in 'should now' have a different meaning but the same spelling as the 'should' in 'should have'. This multiplication of meanings would be a loss in simplicity, although it would permit the 'should' in 'should now' to be simply the past tense of 'shall', used in subordinate clauses, indirect speech, and conditional constructions; in fact, this is precisely what I think it is (see Chapter 3, below). The second problem is that 'You played that exactly as you should have' becomes 'Would that you had played that exactly as you did' which expresses a rather odd sort of idle wish. The 'should'-sentence seems rather to express a satisfaction with the way things turned out, than a wish that things had not turned out differently than they did (whatever that could be). But perhaps there is something in common between the satisfaction expressed by 'You played that as you should have' and the wish expressed by 'You did not play that as you should have' which means 'You should have played that differently than you did.' If so, both sentences could be analysed in terms of the common element. I leave that project to someone else.

In 'A Doubt About Universal Prescriptivism' I argued that, according to the theory of *The Language of Morals*, when I tell someone that it is wrong to punish the innocent I am telling him to make it the case that no one ever does this: and since I know he cannot make this the case, it is an absurd thing to tell him to do. Hare has replied that

> the difficulty . . . is readily diagnosed and removed if we distinguish, much as Mr. Kenny and his predecessors have done, between *directives*, which place the responsibility on the addressee, and *fiats*, which do not (*Analysis* 26.3, January, 1966, p. 68). If we then say that universal prescriptions are fiats, we shall be freed from the absurdity of supposing that when I utter one, I am commanding the person addressed to make it the case that all the singular commands which my universal prescription entails are

obeyed. The most I am doing is uttering a fiat which anybody who, in the circumstances specified in the prescription, did not do the action specified would be failing to satisfy. ('Universal and Past-Tense Prescriptions', p. 165).

But this does not solve the problem if sincerely *prescribing* that something happen is defined in terms of *intending* that it happen, and hence intending to do something to make it happen. I cannot intend that no one at any time (past, present, or future) punish the innocent, and if this is what is required for me to think it is wrong to punish the innocent then it is impossible for me or anyone else to think it wrong. It seems again more promising to analyse 'It is wrong to punish the innocent', not as a universal prescription which entails singular prescriptions in all the persons and all the tenses, but as entailing some judgements expressed in the imperative mood and others expressed in the optative. And since sincere assent to such judgements requires wishing as well as intending, it would be nice if these could be analysed as having a common element so that they were not ultimate and irreducible mental states.

Another point that concerns Hare is the variable temporal reference of future-tense prescriptions. We may observe that the sentence 'You should now play that more softly than you did' will not be used to say exactly the same thing on two different occasions of utterance: each time it is uttered the temporal reference of 'now' will be different. This is, of course, a familiar phenomenon and is a feature of indicative as well as imperative sentences. Hare thinks it presents a special difficulty for prescriptive discourse which can be avoided only by the admission of past-tense prescriptions. He suggests that the 'No Smoking' sign in a railway carriage expresses a command which

> might be held to entail *some* past-tense imperatives, on the ground that a person who is apprehended for breaking the 'No Smoking' rule cannot escape retribution by pleading that nobody can now with point express the rule which he broke. (ibid., pp. 162–3)

If we say 'Do not smoke from now on' he will protest that by smoking in the past he has not disobeyed this future-tense command, and he would be right. But that is not the command he is charged with breaking; the relevant command is the one with which he was issued by the 'No Smoking' sign. His plea that there can be no point in now issuing that command is perfectly correct but completely irrelevant.

The sign told him in the past not to smoke at subsequent times, and he did smoke at those times. Although there is no point in our *now* telling him not to smoke when he did, there was a point in telling him in the past. For this purpose it does not matter whether the injunction expressed by the sign changes as time goes on. If the command it is now used to issue is different from the one it expressed previously, then the smoker is guilty of violating the earlier one and not the later one.

Hare sees that

> a more promising move is to say that the notice always means the same, namely what the person meant who first put it up. *He* was referring to all times in the future and not to any past times. What the offender is punished for is breaking the future-tense commands given in the past by this august person. (ibid., p. 163)

This seems to me correct. Although we can say that the sign told him in the past not to smoke when he did, there can be no point in our telling him now not to have smoked when he did; but if our only concern is with retribution then we shall punish him for doing what the sign told him not to do, and not for doing anything we can now tell him to refrain from doing.

But Hare sees another difficulty. If the authorities of British Rail are asked to state their present requirements, would they require only that the 'No Smoking' signs be obeyed from now on? If so 'they cannot call past breaches breaches of their present requirements' (p. 163). This is true, but not the point at issue. The smoker violated a past requirement, not a present one, and that is what he is to be punished for, if he is to be punished at all. The authorities might decide: 'We no longer require that people refrain from smoking in those carriages and we shall not prosecute those who did smoke when it was forbidden.' In that case it would still be true that the smoker broke a past requirement, but he is no longer to be punished for it. The question whether what he did was in fact forbidden when he did it is logically independent of the question whether he is still to be punished for having done it. The authorities might even say, with regard to certain carriages which have never had 'No Smoking' signs: 'From now on we require that no one smoke in those carriages, and we shall even prosecute those who smoked in them when it was not forbidden.' Such retro-active legislation is to be criticized on the grounds, not that it is illogical or inconsistent, but that it is unfair. For this we do not need past prescriptions.

PRESCRIPTIVE ENTAILMENT

In ordinary indicative logic an argument is deductively valid if and only if it is logically impossible for the premises to be true and the conclusion false. If this definition were applied to arguments with indicative premises and prescriptive conclusions, then all such arguments would be valid. For it is logically impossible that any prescription be true or false; hence *a fortiori* it is logically impossible to have an argument with true indicative premises and a false prescriptive conclusion. So if there is to be such a thing as deductive validity in prescriptive arguments, a validity which some arguments have and others lack, it must obviously be a different sort of validity than the kind with which indicative logic deals. But what sense can it make to speak of two different kinds of validity, in contrast to the *word* 'validity' simply having two different meanings? Consider the sentence 'River-sides and financial institutions are two different kinds of banks.' If the word 'banks' is being *used* in this sentence (in order to talk about banks rather than words) and is not merely *mentioned* (in order to talk about itself) then the proposition expressed by this sentence *must* be false. For suppose the word is used to mean 'financial institutions'; then the proposition will be false because river-sides are not a kind of financial institution. If the word is used to mean 'river-side' then the proposition is false again since financial institutions are not a kind of river-side. And there is nothing left for the word to mean, if it is being used and not mentioned. Of course, if the word is merely being mentioned then the sentence really means 'The word "bank" can mean either "river-side" or "financial institution".' So if we propose that there are different kinds of validity are we merely proposing to use the *word* 'validity' with different meanings, perhaps as unrelated as those of 'river-side' and 'financial institution'? Or are we proposing that there is something in common between the different kinds of validity which justifies applying the word 'validity' in the same sense to both (as there is nothing in common between river-sides and financial institutions which justifies applying the word 'bank' in the same sense to both)?

In what is called *the logic of satisfaction* validity for prescriptive or "mixed" inferences (i.e. inferences which may contain a mixture of statements and prescriptions among their premisses and conclusions) is defined as follows:

> a prescriptive argument is deductively valid if and only if it is logically impossible for the premisses to contain only true statements and/or satisfied prescriptions while the conclusion contains a false statement or an unsatisfied prescription.

For instance, the following argument is deductively valid according to this definition:

(A) 1. Read all the books in the syllabus.
    2. This is a book in the syllabus.

∴ 3. Read this book.

It is logically impossible for the person addressed to satisfy the first premise without satisfying the conclusion if the second premise is true. But for argument (A) to have validity as defined in the logic of satisfaction is simply for the following argument to have plain old-fashioned validity:

(B) 1. The prescription 'Read all the books in the syllabus' is satisfied.
    2. The proposition 'This is a book in the syllabus' is true.

∴ 3. The prescription 'Read this book' is satisfied.

Since the prescriptive 'validity' of argument (A) reduces to the ordinary indicative validity of argument (B), is there any reason to say that they have two kinds of validity? Both arguments are 'valid' in the sense defined in the logic of satisfaction; (B) is merely a special case in which there are no prescriptions to worry about. But this does not seem adequate by itself. We might define a sense of 'mother' as follows: x is a mother if and only if x is either a female parent or the wedding ring of a female parent. Then Queen Elizabeth's wedding ring would count as a 'mother' in the sense defined only because the Queen herself counts as a mother in the ordinary sense. Are there then two kinds of mothers? Well, the Queen and her ring are both 'mothers' in the sense defined; the Queen is just a special case. Or we could define a *third* sense of 'bank' in which 'x is a bank' means 'x is either a river-side or a financial institution'; and then the Bank of England will be just a special case of a 'bank', the side of the Thames being another special case.

Clearly, if the philosophers defending the logic of satisfaction were merely stipulating a sense for the expression 'prescriptive validity' then there would be nothing about which to argue with them: in saying that argument (A) was 'valid' in prescriptive logic they would simply be saying that argument (B) was valid in indicative logic, which is something no one denies. There must be something more important at stake than assigning a new sense to an old word. The defenders of the logic of satisfaction wish to maintain that there is something about our ordinary notion of validity which makes it appropriate to say that (A) is valid in the ordinary sense. Everyone agrees that it is some sort of mistake to agree to read all the books in the syllabus and agree that, say, the *Odyssey* is a book in the syllabus, and yet decline or refuse to read the *Odyssey*. And what can the mistake be if it is not a kind of inconsistency? But it can be an inconsistency only if (A) is a valid argument. Yet this talk of inconsistency seems to amount to no more than the universally accepted claim that the truth of B1 and B2 is inconsistent in the ordinary sense with the truth of B3.

Bernard Williams argues that there is another kind of inconsistency at issue.[5] He considers the 'alleged' inference:

(C) 1. Do x or do Y.
    2. Do not do x.

∴ 3. Do y.

And he acknowledges the validity of the corresponding indicative argument:

(D) 1. The command 'Do x or do y' is obeyed.
    2. The command 'Do not do x' is obeyed.

∴ 3. The command 'Do y' is obeyed.

Thus (C) counts as a valid argument in the logic of satisfaction. But Professor Williams argues that C1 and C2 are inconsistent with each other, whereas D1 and D2 obviously are not. He says that C1 carries a certain permissive presupposition which is revoked in C2:

We can see that the presuppositions of the disjunctive command 'do x or do y' must include permission to do x, and permission to do y; but not, of course, permission to do both x and y . . . ; but the second premiss, 'do not do x', obviously has the force of denying permission to do x. Thus the speaker implicitly gives or admits something with his first utterance, which he withdraws with his second; and this can be construed only as the speaker *changing his mind*, or going back on what he first said . . . we encounter an inconsistency, only interpretable as a change of mind. 'Imperative Inference', pp. 32–3.)

I do not quite understand why he speaks of the command 'do x or do y' as having merely permissive *presuppositions*, for this seems to weaken his case unnecessarily. It is not just presupposed that when someone commands you to do either x or y he is permitting you to do x, in the way that it is presupposed that when someone makes a statement of fact he believes that what he is saying is true. For stating a fact does not involve believing what you state, but commanding an action does involve permitting what you command.

Couching the claim of inconsistency in terms merely of permissive *presuppositions* has led Professor Hare to attack the claim in what I consider to be the wrong place. He has compared these presuppositions with Gricean 'conversational implicatures' which are normally carried by our utterances but which can on occasion be cancelled explicitly.[6] For instance, if someone says 'Jones did either x or y' then he conversationally implies (i.e. leads us to believe) that he does not know which it is that Jones has done; for if he were in a position to make the stronger claim 'Jones did y' we would not expect him to restrict his claim to the weaker one. Suppose that at the time of utterance the speaker did not know whether it was x or y that Jones had done; he may later find out that it was not x, and if his mind is thereby changed it is not in going back on what he earlier thought but in enlarging on it. Although what we conversationally imply by saying 'Jones did either x or y' (namely that we do *not* know which) is logically inconsistent with what we lead people to think by saying 'Jones did not do x' (namely that we *do* know which he did), nevertheless the statement 'Jones did either x or y' is not itself inconsistent with the statement 'Jones did not do x.' And it is the consistency of what is said that is supposed to be at issue, not the consistency of what is conversationally implied by saying it. And if the permissive presuppositions of a series of commands are like the conversational implications of a series of statements, then it is the consistency of the commands that is at issue, not the consistency of the presuppositions.

This talk of presuppositions and implicatures seem to me highly misleading. I can surely state that Jones did either x or y without being ignorant of which it was that Jones did; but I cannot command Jones to do either x or y without, by that very act, permitting him to do x. So if I then proceed to command him not to do x, I have both granted and denied him permission to do x. That is the inconsistency of which Williams complains. To use Hare's own example against him, if I issue an order to the commander of a military convoy to proceed either via Berwick or via Coldstream then *by that very order* I grant him permission to proceed via Coldstream; if I later command him not to go via Coldstream, then I both granted and denied him permission to go via Coldstream, which is a kind of contradiction.

It seems to me that the solution to this puzzle lies in the fact that Williams is dealing with an argument that consists of a series of *commands* rather than, say, recommendations or pieces of advice.

> There are, of course, uses of imperatives other than those of giving commands or orders, and what I say will apply less directly, at least, to some of these other uses. However, it seems obvious that the use of imperatives to give orders or commands is the basic use of imperatives, and if my criticism of the idea of inference in this connection is correct, radical doubts about the idea of imperative inference in general would seem to follow. ('Imperative Inference', pp. 30–1.

It is not altogether clear how it is to be determined that the *basic* use of imperatives is to give commands. Perhaps we are to compare the relative frequencies of the various uses and conclude that imperative sentences are used to issue commands more often than to offer suggestions or to give advice. Such a conclusion would be an interesting, but certainly not obvious, empirical claim since most of us are in a position to offer suggestions more frequently than we have the authority to give orders. But however that may be, there certainly are these other uses of imperative sentences, and what Williams has to say about commands does not apply to some of them. It may be inconsistent to permit someone to do either x or y while commanding him not to do x, but there is no inconsistency if he is merely advised not to do x. For instance, a student who has successfully completed the first-year Mathematics course may be permitted to take either of two second year courses, but if he is contemplating pursuing a Mathematics degree then he might also be advised not to take the course intended for engineers. There is no inconsistency whatever in advising or recommending that someone not do what you have already permitted him to do.

It may be thought that it is impossible to intend to do either x or y, while at the same time intending not to do x, on the ground that if someone intends to do either x or y then he has not yet made up his mind which it is he intends to do. Now it is true that 'A intends to do either x or y' does not entail 'either A intends to do x or A intends to do y'. But it does not have to; it is enough that the entailment go the other way. For 'A intends to do y' entails 'either A intends to do x or A intends to do y' which in turn does seem to entail 'A intends to do either x or y'. Thus, one may intend to do either x or y (by virtue of intending to do y) while simultaneously intending not to do x. Consequently, one may consistently assent to the two *prescriptions* 'do either x or y' and 'do not do x'.

What makes Williams' argument a valid one about *commands* is that to command someone not to do x is do more than merely prescribe to him that he not do x. Perhaps it is too strong to say that it is both to prescribe he not do it and to *threaten* him with punishment if he does, for that seems to imply hostility on the part of the person giving the command. But the commander at least *commits* himself to taking punitive measures against someone who does what he commands not to be done. On the other hand, if he commands someone to do either x or y then he permits that person to do x by explicitly committing himself not to punish that person if he does x. For this reason the logic of commands or orders resembles deontic logic in being 'three-valued'. In deontic logic an action x is either obligatory ('Ox'), permitted ('–O–x'), or it is obligatory not to do it ('O–x'); in command logic an action is either commanded ('Cx'), permitted ('–C–x'), or forbidden ('C–x').

This extra committment is a feature of commands and not of prescriptions as such. So although command logic is not analogous to ordinary two-valued indicative logic, nothing so far prevents 'advice logic' or 'suggestion logic' from having rules analogous to two-valued logic. If there is such a thing as 'practical reasoning' it does not consist in addressing to oneself a series of commands, and so there is no reason to think that Williams' strictures apply to it. Neither is there, for instance, any inconsistency in *agreeing* to do either x or y while also agreeing not to do x.

A. J. P. KENNY AND THE LOGIC OF SATISFACTORINESS

In ordinary indicative logic a valid argument is one in which truth is necessarily preserved from premisses to conclusion. Prescriptions do not have a truth-value since their job is to say what to do, not what is the case.

> Now if we are to ask in what sense practical reasoning necessitates its conclusion, we must ask: what is the value which rules of practical reasoning have as their purpose to preserve in the way in which truth is the value preserved by rules of theoretical reasoning? (Anthony Kenny, 'Practical Reasoning and Rational Appetite' in *Will, Freedom and Power*, Blackwell, 1975, p. 71)

Mr. Kenny gives this value the name 'satisfactoriness', and I think its meaning can be expláined as follows. Let us grant that to have a desire is 'to say-in-one's-heart an imperative', so that an imperative sentence will be the linguistic expression of a desire, in the way that an indicative sentence is the linguistic expression of a belief. Any imperative whose satisfaction will bring about what is desired by some person (including, trivially, the imperative which expresses that person's desire) will be *considered* 'satisfactory' by that person, at least for that purpose, although it may be considered unsatisfactory for other purposes if its satisfaction conflicts with other things that are desired.

What are the rules of inference which preserve satisfactoriness from premisses to conclusion in a piece of valid practical reasoning? According to Kenny, 'the logic of satisfactoriness is the mirror image of the logic of satisfaction' (p. 82). That is, the fiat 'Let q be the case' entails 'Let p be the case' if and only if the material conditional 'If p is the case then q is the case' is tautological. But this has what seems to me a very awkward consequence. Since the contradiction 'p is the case and not-p is the case' logically entails 'p is the case', it follows that any fiat whatever 'Let p be the case' entails in Kenny's logic a contradictory fiat 'Let p be the case and let not-p be the case.' If we are casting about for values which are to be preserved in practical inferences, we should at least make sure that the resulting logic does not commit us to desiring logically impossible states of affairs if we desire anything at all.

He admits that his logic has consequences which appear odd on the surface:

For instance, in this logic the inference 'Kill the conspirators; Brutus is a conspirator; so kill Brutus' is invalid. But this result, properly understood, is perfectly correct: the order 'Kill the conspirators' has not been fully obeyed by someone who obeys the order 'Kill Brutus' unless Brutus is the only conspirator, which the premisses do not entitle us to conclude. (ibid. p. 83)

It is true that if Brutus is not the only conspirator then someone who agrees to kill all the conspirators will not, just by killing Brutus, do *all* that he agrees to do. But why should it be otherwise in order for the inference to be valid? Surely, if it is desireable to kill all the cospirators, and Brutus is a conspirator, then it is desireable to kill Brutus, although that is not *all* that is desireable. Someone might object that the word 'desire*able*' introduces an 'opaque' context where we cannot validly deduce the desireability of killing Brutus from the identity of Brutus with one of the conspirators together with the desireability of killing all the conspirators. Certainly, 'It is desir*ed* that all the conspirators be killed' and 'Brutus is a conspirator' do not entail 'It is desir*ed* that Brutus be killed.' But this is not the real issue, for Kenny would say the same thing about the inference 'Kill Brutus and kill Cassius; so kill Brutus'; he would deny its validity on the ground that to kill Brutus is not thereby to *fully* satisfy the prescription 'Kill Brutus and kill Cassius.' But why should it? If it is desireable to kill both Brutus and Cassius, how can it fail to be desireable to kill Brutus?

Kenny seems committed to maintaining that it is not self-contradictory to say 'Kill the conspirators; Brutus is a conspirator; but do not kill Brutus', or to say 'Kill Brutus and kill Cassius; but do not kill Brutus' and this is just too far-fetched. It requires that someone who said the latter, for example, would not be prescribing both that Brutus be killed and that he not be killed. But nothing can be more obvious than that someone who prescribes that Brutus be killed and that Cassius be killed *is* prescribing (among other things) that Brutus be killed, and that he cannot go on to prescribe that Brutus not be killed without contradicting himself. This *by itself* shows that the prescription to kill Brutus and Cassius logically entails the prescription to kill Brutus; the fact that the conjunctive premise has not been fully obeyed by someone who obeys only one of the prescriptive conjuncts, is irrelevant. Now this argument that I have just given relies on the claim that the negation of 'Do A' is 'Do not do A.' This has been denied (e.g. by Lars Bergström; 'Imperatives and

Contradiction', *Mind*, 1970). The proper contradictory of 'Do A' has been alleged to be 'You need not do A', while the negation of 'Do not do A' is 'You may do A.' This may be true of *commands*, which are more than just prescriptions, but they certainly are not true of advice or suggestions. For instance, intending to do something, which is at least a necessary condition for sincere assent to any prescription, is *not* inconsistent with thinking that one need not do it, any more than intending not to do something is inconsistent with thinking that one may do it. 'You need not' and 'You may' seem rather to be the natural negations of 'You must' and 'You must not.'

Consider the inference: 'Put your parachute on and jump out; therefore, jump out.' If it is desireable to put on your parachute and jump out, then it is desireable to jump out; of course, it is not desireable *just* to jump out, i.e. to jump out *and not* put on your parachute, but no one expected otherwise. If it is *true* that you have put on your parachute and jumped out then it is true that you have jumped out; but no one would conclude that it is true *just* that you have jumped out, or that you have jumped out and *not* put on your parachute.

I would maintain that no argument which is valid in the logic of satisfaction fails to preserve satisfactoriness or desireability from premisses to conclusion. What, then, about the old favourite: 'Post the letter; therefore, post the letter or burn it'? I claim that if it is desireable that the letter be posted then it is also desireable that it be either posted or burned. 'But if someone burns the letter then he brings it about that the letter is either posted or burned, although he does *not* bring about anything desireable.' This objection is beside the point. From the desireability of bringing it about that the letter is posted it does not follow that it is desireable to bring it about *by just any means at all* that the letter is either posted or burned. Perhaps the following analogy will help to clear up the issue. If 'The earth is a planet' is true, then 'The earth is either a planet or a star' is also true; and 'The earth is a star' entails 'The earth is either a planet or a star', which is true; but to conclude that 'The earth is a star' is true is simply to commit the fallacy of affirming the consequent. Similarly, if 'Post the letter' is satisfactory or desireable, and it entails 'Either post the letter or burn it' (as it does in the logic of satisfaction) then it too is satisfactory, since satisfactoriness is preserved from premise to conclusion; and 'Burn the letter' also entails 'Either post the letter or burn it', which we may suppose to be satisfactory. But to conclude that 'Burn the letter' must be satisfactory because it entails 'Either post the letter or burn it' which is satisfactory, is surely just as fallacious as to infer that 'The earth is a star' is true because it entails 'The earth is either a planet or a star' which is true.

Kenny has tried to argue that the inference from 'Let p be the case' to 'Let p and q be the case' is valid by attempting to make out that someone who assented to the former and dissented from the latter would be guilty of an inconsistency.

> For if someone has expressed his current wants adequately in a goal-fiat, then there *is* something inconsistent in his refusing to welcome a fiat which is derivable from it in the logic of satisfactoriness. If my *only* want is to have the door open, why should I object if someone opens the door and smashes the window? Of course there is something insane in the idea of having only a single want of that kind; and the reason I would object in the case in point is that I don't want the window smashed. But if that is among my wants, then it should be included in the goal-fiat from which the practical reason starts. (ibid., p. 91)

One may as well say that if my *only* belief is that Paris is in France then I should not object to its entailing that Paris is in France and San Francisco is in Germany, and that if the conclusion is inconsistent with other beliefs I hold then I should include those beliefs among the premises from which my reasoning starts. There is clearly no reason why I should have to state everything I believe merely in order to state *something* I believe, and we have been offered no reason why we should have to specify *all* our goals in a fiat in order merely to specify some of them. If a proposition is true then its conjuction with all other true propositions is also true; and if a goal-fiat is satisfactory then its conjunction with all other satisfactory goal-fiats should be satisfactory as well. This requirement is not met in Kenny's logic, but is met in the logic of satisfaction. Of course, what is preserved from premises to conclusion in the logic of satisfaction is a *limited* satisfactoriness; for a goal-fiat to be satisfactory in this logic is for its satisfaction to bring about *something* desireable. In Kenny's logic a goal-fiat is not satisfactory unless its fulfilment brings about *everything* desireable. He argues that

> in practical inference it is only the logic of satisfactoriness which is *conclusive*, in the sense of ensuring that the conclusion has the

value that the reasoning aims at, namely the satisfaction of the reasoner's wants. The logic of satisfaction – reasoning to necessary conditions for satisfaction – is never conclusive in the sense of ensuring the arrival of what is wanted. Having carried out a piece of practical reasoning to necessary conditions, and put the conclusion into action, the reasoner cannot then rest secure in the confidence that what he has done will bring about the state of affairs he wants: there may be *more* that he has to do in order to achieve his goals. (ibid., p. 89)

It is true that the logic of satisfaction does not ensure that putting into action the conclusion of practical inference will bring about the satisfaction of *all* the reasoner's desires, but I don't see why any piece of practical reasoning should be required to accomplish this feat. Kenny has so far offered us no reason to believe that the value we actually seek to preserve from premisses to conclusion in a practical inference is the satisfaction of all our desires at once.

P. T. GEACH ON THE LOGIC OF SATISFACTION

In the logic of satisfaction a set of indicative premisses is said to entail a prescriptive conclusion if and only if it is logically impossible for the premisses to be true and the conclusion unsatisfied. In *The Language of Morals* (OUP, 1952) Hare had written that 'No imperative conclusion can be validly drawn from a set of premisses which does not contain at least one imperative" (p. 28). However, on p. 35 he himself provided a counter-example to this rule as it is stated. He began by considering the inference:

1. Go to the largest grocer in Oxford.
2. Grimbly Hughes is the largest grocer in Oxford.

∴3. Go to Grimbly Hughes.

With regard to an earlier example consisting of indicative sentences he had written that a 'more complex form of the inference is arrived at by taking away the major premiss from its proper place, and adding it to the conclusion inside an hypothetical clause' (p. 34). Applying this transformation to the present example yields the one-premise inference:

2. Grimbly Hughes is the largest grocer in Oxford.

∴.4. If go to the largest grocer in Oxford then go to Grimbly Hughes.

Since (4) is ungrammatical as it stands Hare rewrote it so that it read: 'If you want to go to the largest grocer in Oxford, go to Grimbly Hughes. Professor Geach, in 'Imperative and Deontic Logic'[7] rendered it: 'Either do not go to the largest grocer in Oxford or go to Grimbly Hughes', and commented that

> The conclusion here is undoubtedly imperative [although] it may indeed seem to be vacuous as an imperative, because, as things are in Oxford, you cannot help fulfilling it, whatever you do. (Ibid., p. 276)

In 'Geach on Murder and Sodomy'[8] Hare wrote that

> though Geach has certainly produced examples of valid inferences from non-evaluative premises to evaluative conclusions, the conclusions are all logically complex and the bearing of his arguments on the thesis of moral autonomy remains unclear . . . (by 'logically simple' I mean 'not containing any logical connectives'). (Ibid., pp. 468–9)

What examples such as these succeed in showing is that it is a very simple procedure to derive prescriptions from statements of fact, but not one that gives us any help at all in deciding what to do. You begin with a tautological prescription which logically cannot be unfulfilled, such as 'Either go to Grimbly Hughes or do not go to Grimbly Hughes.' Then modify the prescription so that it *can* logically be contravened – but *not* if certain facts obtain. In this case we modify the prescription to read 'Either to go to Grimbly Hughes or do not go to the largest grocer in Oxford', which can go unfulfilled but not if the indicative premise 'Grimbly Hughes is the largest grocer in Oxford' is true. You then have a valid argument in the logic of satisfaction. But the price to be paid for all such arguments is that, given the facts of the case, the conclusion has no bearing whatever on the question what to do. We do not deliberate about whether to do what is unavoidable, and in this case there is no way that we can avoid doing what the conclusion prescribes if the factual premise is true. On the other hand, if the action is one whose avoidance is not logically precluded by the facts then no true statement will provide a logically conclusive reason for performing the action, since it will be possible without logical inconsistency to agree with the factual statement while refusing to give assent to the prescription. Thus, the factual premise 'You would not like it if someone set fire to you' does not logically entail the prescriptive conclusion 'Do not set fire to others' since there is obviously no logical impossibility in doing to others what you would not like them to do to you.

Geach's recent attempt to derive a non-vacuous prescription from solely factual premises can also be seen to fail. In his article 'Again the Logic of "Ought"'[9] he constructs the following argument:

1. If Evan promises Uncle Dewi that he will do something, then he will do it.
2. If Evan utters sentence W in certain circumstances he will be promising Undle Dewi that he will do something that he ought not to do.
3. No one ought to do something which he ought not to do.
∴.4. If Evan utters sentence W in the given circumstances he will do something which he ought not to do.
∴.5. Evan ought not to utter sentence W.

According to Geach, (4) is derived from the factual premisses (1) and (2), while (5) is derived from (4) together with the vacuous 'ought'-statement (3). He claims therefore to have derived (5) solely from factual premisses and a tautological evaluative thesis. But premise (1) is not factual, it is evaluative. We can see this by constructing a much simpler argument which has all the relevant features of Geach's original. Premise (1), together with the factual premise

6. Evan promised Uncle Dewi yesterday that he would do something he ought not to do before the day was out,

entails the evaluative conclusion

7. Yesterday Evan did something which he ought not to have done.

It might be thought that (6) is the real culprit if it means that there is some act A which Evan promised to do, and Evan ought not to do A.

But the game would be over very quickly if that is what it meant. We can make it last just a bit longer if we take (6) to be *oratio obligua* for

> 6'. Even promised Uncle Dewi yesterday: 'I will do something which I ought not to do, before the day is out.'

The trouble now is that in order to assure ourselves that (1) is true, we must be satisfied that Evan kept the promise he made yesterday. And we cannot do this unless we are satisfied that Evan did something wrong yesterday. It is irrelevant that Evan and Uncle Dewi agree that he did something wrong; that would yield only a factual conclusion about what the two of them *think* Evan ought not to have done. In order for *us* to agree that he kept his promise, we must *ourselves* agree that what he did was wrong. Suppose we ask them what it was whose performance fulfilled the promise, and Evan replies: 'I made a point of not tipping the cab driver.' If we do not think this wrong, we will not agree that Evan has done anything which fulfils his promise. The fact that we must evaluate his actions yesterday in order to decide whether he kept his promise shows that (1) is not a purely factual premise.

QUIXOTIC LOGIC

Whether the rightness or wrongness of an action provides a logically conclusive reason either for doing it or for not doing it depends entirely upon what we are saying when we call an action right or wrong. If in saying that an action is wrong I am, among other things, issuing a prescription which logically entails the prescription that I not do the action, then of course I am committed on pain of inconsistency to agreeing not to do it once I have agreed that it is wrong. But if to call an action wrong is merely to state a fact about it, and not to issue any prescription, then its being wrong will not provide logically conclusive grounds for not doing it. For *either* it makes no sense at all to speak of prescriptive conclusions following logically from factual premises, *or* the sense in which prescriptions can follow from propositions is that defined by the logic of satisfaction. The only other candidate for a prescriptive logic was Kenny's version of the logic of satisfactoriness, and that was ruled out because it had the intolerable consequence that *any* prescription 'Let p be the case' logically entailed the contradictory prescription 'Let p be the case and let not-p be the case.' Now no one would wish to maintain that it is logically impossible to do what is morally wrong; but if an act's being wrong does not preclude it from being performed, then the 'truth' of the judgement that it is wrong will not prevent the prescription that it not be done from being contravened or violated. In that case the moral judgement does not entail the prescription, so that no one is logically committed to assenting to the prescription once he has accepted the moral judgement as true. If moral judgements were a conjunction of statements and prescriptions then again the statement component by itself would not entail the complete moral judgement; it would be perfectly consistent to agree with the factual part without assenting to *both* the factual *and* the prescriptive parts.

A person who defined 'ought' so that 'ought' – judgements both followed from statements of fact and entailed singular prescriptions would be like A. N. Prior's logician who defined a sentential connective 'tonk' in such a way that any proposition 'p' entailed 'p tonk q' for any 'q' whatever, and 'p tonk q' entailed 'q'; thus enabling any proposition to be validly deduced from any other.[10] Now it is commonly assumed that we are at perfect liberty to give an abitrary symbol any meaning we please simply by defining it to mean what we wish. If we are willing to face the consequences we may, for instance, define the word 'squound' so that it means 'figure which is both round and square at the same time'. The consequence of defining the word in this way is that it turns out to be impossible for there to be anything to which it could be correctly applied. However, if we are willing to pay the price then we may give the word such a meaning that it can never apply to anything.

But the matter is not as simple as that. Suppose we attempt to assign a meaning to the word 'tonk' by stipulating that when it is placed between two sentences, the resulting compound sentence expresses that proposition which both follows from the proposition expressed by the first component sentence and entails the proposition expressed by the second. Thus, the sentence 'Grass is green tonk snow is white' expresses that proposition which both follows from 'Grass is green' and entails 'Snow is white.' But there is no such proposition for the compound sentence to express, and so it follows that the word 'tonk' cannot acquire meaning simply by being assigned to the role of forming sentences which express it. If we are going to stipulate that the role of a certain word is to form sentences which express propositions of a given description, we should at least check to see whether any proposition could ever fit the description.

If talk of propositions is thought to be in some way objectionable, we may arrive at the same conclusion by a different route. Suppose we attempt to define the English word 'tonk' by its role in inferences, and use Wilfrid Sellars' device of dot-quotation[11] to call any word in any language a "·tonk·" if it plays the same role. Thus, any word-token will be a ·tonk· if, for example, when placed between a ·Grass is green· and a ·Snow is white· the result is a sentence-token satisfying the two conditions of following logically from any ·Grass is green· and entailing any ·Snow is white·. We might call such a sentence-token a ·Grass is green tonk snow is white·. But since no sentence-token could ever satisfy these conditions, it follows that no word could play the role of forming sentence-tokens that do satisfy them, which is just to say that no word could be a ·tonk·. Hence we could never succeed in giving a word the meaning required of a ·tonk·, contrary to the assumption that we can give a word any meaning we like simply by stipulating that it shall play a role of a particular description. We may certainly define a ·tonk· to be any word that plays this role, but we cannot take a word and simply by definition make it play that role if it is a role that it is logically impossible for any word to play. And if the meaning of a word is the role it plays, then we cannot by stipulation make a word mean something which it is impossible for anything to mean.

The same problem arises if we try to define 'ought' in a like manner. We might say that its meaning is determined by its role in facilitating valid inferences from statements of fact to singular pre-scriptions, and call any word in any language an ·ought· if it had a similar function. A word will then be an ·ought· just in case the result of concatenating it with other words in a certain way is a sentence-token which satisfies the two conditions of entailing singular prescrip-tions of the form ·Do X· and following from statements of the form ·X is an act of type F·, where 'F' is a descriptive predicate. But, by the transitivity of entailment, no sentence-token could satisfy these conditions; and the result of this definition, as with the definition of a squound, is merely to set the requirements for being an ·ought· so high that it is logically impossible for anything to meet them. Since no word could be an ·ought· it follows again that it is impossible for any word to have the meaning required of an ·ought· contrary to the assumption that we can make a word, by stipulation, mean anything we like.

So, where the facts of the case do not make it impossible to avoid doing a certain action they do not provide what can be called a *logically* conclusive reason to do it, and there is no logical inconsistency in acknowledging the facts and refusing to do it. The person who acknowledges that he would not like it if someone set fire to him just for fun, but dissents from the prescription not to set fire to others, is not illogical, he is immoral; for although the fact that he would not like it done to himself does not provide a logically conclusive reason not to do it to others, it provides a pretty strong reason nevertheless.

3 What Is It To Call a Consideration a Reason To Do Something?

The aim of this chapter is to show that, although factual considerations provide reasons to do various things, it is not a fact *about* any consideration that it does so. And I try to prove this by showing that to *call* a consideration a reason to do something is not to *state* a fact about it. Suppose, for instance, that when we tell a person *that* he is not to smoke in the Chemistry laboratory we are simply telling him *not to* smoke there; then it will not be a fact about anyone that he is not to smoke in the Chemistry Laboratory, for to say that he is not to smoke there will not be to state fact but to issue an injunction forbidding him to do so. And to forbid someone to do a thing is not to say anything true or false about him. The burden of the present argument, therefore, will be to show that we are not stating a fact about a consideration when we say it is a reason to do something, but are doing another linguistic job instead; in particular; issuing a prescription of a certain sort.

'WHY?' - QUESTIONS

Now there seems to be at least one uncontroversial claim about reasons, namely that they are what we do or could give in answer to 'Why?'-questions. Anyone who asks 'Why?' with regard to something is enquiring after the reason for it, and we have not told him the reason for it unless we have said something which could answer a possible 'Why?'-question. There are different kinds of 'Why?-questions and corresponding to them are different kinds of reasons. Two of these sorts of reasons, which I wish to call 'explanation' and 'justification' are worth comparing and contrasting. I take something to be an explanation when it could be used in order to answer a factual question asking why something is the case or why some state of affairs obtains, such as 'Why did the pipes freeze last night?' or 'Why did Marc Antony desert his soldiers at the Battle of Actium?.' On the other hand, I take something to be a justification if it answers a practical question asking why an action is to be done or avoided. It does not really matter whether the words 'explanation' and 'justification' are ordinarily used in precisely this way, and I have no interest in showing that they are; what is important is the distinction, which I use these words to mark, between answering a factual 'Why?'-question and answering a practical 'Why?'-question. The former can be represented as having the form: 'Why is it the case that P?', where the letter P stands for some sentence expressing a proposition which is either true or false; to answer such a question we must be able to say something of the form 'P because Q', where Q also stands for a sentence expressing a proposition which is either true or false. The answer to a practical 'Why'-question must also be able to take the form 'P because Q', but this time P stands for a sentence expressing a prescription which can, by definition, be neither true or false. This is the distinction to which I wish to draw attention.

If Antony ever put to himself at Actium the question 'Why not stay and fight Octavian?' then he evidently took to be sufficient reason the fact that Cleopatra's ship was retreating from the scene of the battle and that he might not see her again. Now an historian might use the fact that Antony saw Cleopatra's ship retreating and wanted to be with her in order to answer the question 'Why did Antony desert?'; but the facts that provide a sufficient answer to the historian's question do not on that account provide a sufficient answer to Antony's question. Someone watching the proceedings might make the prediction 'Antony will leave his soldiers because he sees Cleopatra's ship retreating', where both of the sentences 'Antony will leave' and 'He sees Cleopatra's ship retreating' express true propositions. But an answer to Antony's question would be, for example, 'Don't stay and fight Octavian, for Cleopatra's ship is retreating', where the sentence 'Don't stay and fight Octovian' expresses no proposition which is either true or false.

The difference between the two kinds of answers may be pretty obvious, but what is perhaps enlightening is the fact that the *form* of an answer to a 'Why?'-question is structurally related to the question it answers in much the same way whether it be a factual or a practical question. Suppose someone asks why the pipes froze last night, and we tell him that the windows were left open. Now when someone *asks* why the pipes froze, the way to answer is by *saying* why they froze; and we have answered his question correctly if the window's having been left open is in fact why the pipes froze. Of course we may say that this is only one reason why they froze and not the unique reason; another reason might be the fact that the temperature outside was – 10 degrees. But we do not think it necessary to mention all the background circumstances of the causal field which are understood to be more or less standing conditions and which don't differentiate last night from any other night when the pipes might have frozen but didn't. We cite only the distinctive feature that was absent the other nights and present last night and is sufficient, given the rest of the causal field, to make the pipes freeze. If these is more than one distinctive feature but none of them individually is sufficient in the presence of the standing conditions to cause the pipes to freeze, then each of them is a contributing reason.

Let us suppose that the only remarkable feature about last night was the fact that the windows were left open. Then if someone asks why the pipes froze we might say 'because the windows were left open', or simply 'the windows were left open'. However, merely to say that the windows were left open is not yet to say that their having been left open is a reason for anything. Of course, these are circumstances (such as the ones mentioned) in which we can assert the proposition that the pipes froze because the windows were left open simply by uttering the sentence 'The windows were left open.' But equally, we can assert any proposition whatever just by uttering the word 'yes' if we have been asked the right question beforehand. What I am interested in is the proposition we assert when we say why something is the case, not the sentence we use to assert it. What I wish to maintain is that if the windows' having been left open really is the reason why the pipes froze, then it must be true to say 'The pipes froze because the windows were left open.'

This may appear to be trivial point, but it has an interesting consequence. And this is the principle that in order to say why something, e.g. the fact that P, is the case, we must be able to say something with the logical form 'P because Q' or, what is the same thing, 'The reason why P is that Q.' This merely reflects the way in which the words 'why' and 'because' are related: to say of the fact that the windows were left open that it is *why* the pipes froze, or that it is the *reason* why they froze, is simply another way of saying that they froze *because* the windows were left open. What we have then is a compound sentence consisting of two shorter sentences, 'The pipes froze' and 'The windows were left open', joined together with the word 'because'. This word is a sentential connective since it is used to connect two sentences together to make a third. It is admittedly not a truth–functional connective since the truth of the proposition expressed by the compound sentence cannot be assessed solely by a consideration of the truth or falsity to the propositions expressed by the constituent sentences. Yet any proposition of the form 'P because Q', entails a corresponding proposition of the form 'P and Q', which in turn entails both 'P' and 'Q'. This is obvious from the fact that anyone who said that the pipes froze because the windows were left open, and the went on to deny either that the pipes froze or that the windows were left open, would be contradicting himself. It follows from this that 'P because Q' is true only if both 'P' and 'Q' are true. And certainly a necessary condition of 'P and Q' and hence 'P because Q', having any truth-value at all is that both 'P' and 'Q' have truth-values. If they both have truth-values but one or both are false then 'P because Q' is false. If one of them has no truth value, because, e.g. it is a command or some other form of prescription, then the compound sentence does not express anything true or false in addition to what the remaining component already expresses. For instance, to say either 'Don't stick pins into the cat, because you wouldn't like pins stuck into you' or 'The reason not to stick pins into the cat is that you wouldn't like pins stuck into you' is to say at least two things: it is to prescribe not sticking pins into the cat *and* to state that you would not like them stuck into you. Again, it is to say more than this but the remainder does not concern us here. Since the component sentence 'Don't stick pins into the cat' does not express anything that is either true or false, the only truth or falsehood expressed by the compound sentence is that expressed by the remaining component: 'You would not like pins stuck into you.'

Let us now consider Antony trying to decide whether to leave his ship and abandon his soldiers in order to catch up with Cleopatra. And let me make it clear just what I wish to imagine him deciding here. If he could sincerely think it wrong to leave and yet decide to leave anyway, then the question 'Would it be wrong of me to leave?' is not the one I am interested in, since he could answer it without thereby deciding what to do. Or, if he could acknowledge it to be in his best interest to leave and nevertheless decide to stay out of concern for the welfare of his soldiers, then again the question 'Would it be prudent of me to leave?' is not what we are to imagine him asking. What I have in mind is the case where he finally asks himself simply 'Shall I leave or not?', and to answer this question he must *decide* either to leave or to stay. He may well ask these other questions in the course of making up his mind, but he has not answered this last question until he has left off *discovering* what is the case, and instead turned to *deciding* what to do.

Now instead of the historian's question why Antony did not stay with his soldiers, let us examine the agent's question 'Why not stay with my soldiers?' or, in other words, 'What reason is there not to stay with my soldiers?.' Since Antony is contemplating two courses of action, there are two questions he might put to himself, 'Why stay and fight?' and 'Why leave the ship?.' Someone might answer the first question by saying: 'because the soldiers will fight better, and hence be in less danger, if they can see that their commanding officer has not lost faith in them'. Someone else might answer the second question by saying: 'because Cleopatra is abandoning the fight and if you don't leave now you may never see her again'. Once more, anyone who thinks that these are answers to Antony's questions must be able to say that they are by filling in the blank preceding the word 'because': it must be possible to say 'Stay with your soldiers because . . .' or 'Leave the ship because . . .'. And the resulting sentences must be synonymous with the claims 'The reason for you to stay is that your soldiers will be in less danger if you do' and 'The reason for you to leave is that you may never see Cleopatra again if you don't.' They must mean this because you have not answered Antony when he asks '*What* is the reason for me to stay (or go)?' until you have said of some fact that *it* is the reason for him to stay or go.

THE PRESCRIPTIVE USE OF 'SHOULD'

The point of importance seems to me to be this. Antony is wondering whether or not to stay with his soldiers, and if so, why, and if not, why not. Suppose that he asks 'Shall I stay?' and we answer 'yes'; he then asks 'Why?' and we point to the obvious fact that his soldiers depend on him, and say 'that is why'. Now the sentence 'That is why' can certainly tolerate expansion. If someone overhearing only the last fragment of this conversation were to ask 'That is why what?', we ought to be able to tell him. We could certainly tell him if it had been a question of fact that we were discussing. If he had overheard us referring to the fact that the windows were left open and saying 'that is why', we could have answered his question 'Why what?' by saying 'That is why the pipes froze.' The obvious thing to say in the present case, with regard to the fact that the safety of Antony's soldiers depends to a large extent on his continued presence, is 'That is the reason why he should stay.' And to say to Antony 'The fact that your soldiers would be safer is the reason why you should stay' is just to say 'You should stay because your soldiers would be safer.'

However, this can be so only if the judgement expressed here by 'You should stay' has no truth-value. And the reason is this. When Antony asks himself 'What shall I do?' he is wondering what to do, not what is the case. Of course, he will want to find out the facts of the situation *before* making up his mind to follow one course of action rather than another; but deciding what to do requires something more than discovering what is the case. When he asks 'Shall I stay?' he is not asking for a prediction about what he will end up doing, but advice on what to do. Since he is not asking a factual question, it follows that we cannot be stating a fact by answering 'yes'. Instead we are prescribing that he stay. The prescription need not be specifically a command; it could be simply a piece of advice, a suggestion, or a plea. If he then asks 'Why?', he cannot be asking why some fact obtains, because we have not said that any fact obtains. So if we are to answer his non-factual 'Why?'-question by saying 'You should stay because your soldiers will be in less danger if you do', then the sentence 'You should stay' cannot in this context be used to state a fact. For if it were used to state a fact, then the whole 'because'-sentence would be used to say why that fact obtained. But since he was not asking why any fact obtained, such a reply on our part would not answer his question. The 'because'-sentence can be used to answer his question only if 'you should stay' is not used to state a fact and does not express anything with a truth-value. And since 'P because Q' has a truth-value only if both 'P' and 'Q' have truth-values, it follows that if the 'because'-sentence is to be used to answer Antony's question then the judgement it expresses cannot have a truth-value either.

What then is expressed by the sentence 'You should stay' if not something with a truth-value? I think that 'should' is being used here simply as the form which 'shall' takes in indirect discourse. For instance, the OED says that, among other things, 'should' is 'used in indirect reported utterances, or other statements relating to past time, where "shall" would be used if the time referred to were present'. Thus, if Antony wondered whether to go after Cleopatra, we can report the question he thereby put to himself in two different ways. We can use direct discourse and say 'He asked "Shall I go after Cleopatra?."' But with indirect discourse we can get away without quoting his actual words, or even implying that he uttered any. In that case, the OED tells us to change 'shall' to 'should' and say 'He asked whether he should go after Cleopatra.' This seems straightforward enough; if someone asks 'What shall I do?' we can report his utterance in indirect speech by saying 'He asked what he should do', which in this context clearly means nothing more than 'He asked what to do.' Given this use of 'should', for Antony to wonder whether he should go is just for him to wonder whether to go: and it follows that if we are to answer his question by telling him that he should not go, then we must simply be telling him (advising, urging, etc.) not to go – and are not stating any fact. Otherwise we should not be answering the question he asked, which was not a question of fact. It is not really surprising that here we should have two different but synonymous sentences, 'He wondered whether he should go' and 'He wondered to go'; for in cases where the subject of the indirect question is the same as that of the main verb it is optional whether to include in the indirect question a reference to its subject. And by choosing an infinitive construction or a modal auxiliary we can take either option. But if Antony had asked 'What shall *we* do?' we would have no choice in rendering his question indirectly but to say 'He asked what they should do'.

A famous, if somewhat archaic, example of this transformation occurs in the story of Adam's disobedience as it appears in the *Authorized Edition*. God's injunction is first reported directly: 'And the Lord commanded the man, saying: . . . But of the tree of the knowledge of good and evil, thou shalt not eat of it' (*Genesis* 2: 16–17). In modern English the sentence with 'thou shalt not eat of it' would be rendered by the simple command 'But do not eat of the tree of the knowledge of good and evil.' When God expels Adam and Eve from the Garden of Eden he again reports his command directly by saying 'thou . . . hast eaten of the tree, of which I commanded thee, saying, Thou shalt not eat of it' (*Genesis* 3: 17). Earlier, when he first confronted them with their breach of his command, he reported it indirectly, asking 'Hast thou eaten of the tree, whereof I commanded thee that thou shouldest not eat?' (*Genesis* 3: 11). In the *Revised Standard Edition* this is translated 'Have you eaten of the tree of which I commanded you not to eat?.' Obviously, 'shalt' and

'shouldest' are used here simply to express direct and indirect commands respectively.

Now once we are allowed to say in this prescriptive and non-factual
sense of 'should' that Antony asked himself why he should stay, we
can answer this question by saying that he should stay *because* his
men would be safer, which is not to state anything either true or false
except the fact that his men would be safer if he stayed. To tell him
that this fact is the reason why he should stay is not to state a further
fact *about* the fact that his men would be safer: it is to tell him to stay
and fight because his men would be safer. And of course for Antony
to agree that he should, in this sense, stay behind with his men is
just for him to agree to stay behind, which he cannot sincerely do
without thereby resolving or intending to stay behind. There may be
other senses of 'should' in which the sentence 'You should stay
behind' is used to say something true or false. But I have no idea
what they could be, and none of them is relevant to this issue. For it is
only in the prescriptive sense of 'should' that anyone who asks 'What
shall I do?' is asking what he should do, and therefore it is only in this
sense that we can answer his question by telling him what he should
do. For if we were stating a fact by saying to Antony 'You should stay
behind' then he would say to us: 'That may be true, but I was not
asking what I should do in that sense; I was not asking a question of
fact at all. I was asking what to do.'

Now although it is not a *fact* that Antony should stay because his
soldiers would be safer (since it is neither true nor false), it certainly
does not follow that the fact that his soldiers would be safer is not the
reason why he should stay. To tell him why he should stay is to fill the
blank in the sentence-form 'You should stay because . . . .' As far as
the *form* of the answer is concerned, any indicative sentence could
provide the filler, and none of the resulting sentences would have
more truth than any other (provided, I suppose, that the blank was
always filled with a sentence expressing a true proposition). We could
say 'You should stay because $2 + 2 = 4$' or '. . . because Plato was a
philosopher'. But no one is likely to offer these as answers to
Antony's question 'Why should I stay?', since no one really thinks
that these facts are the reasons why he should stay. But to tell him
that they are not the reasons is not to state a further fact about them;
it is just to affirm the external negation of, e.g. the judgement 'You
should stay because $2 + 2 = 4$.' It is to say 'You should not stay just
because $2 + 2 = 4$' where this is meant to be compatible with both

'You should stay, but not because 2 + 2 = 4' and 'You should not stay even though 2 + 2 = 4.'

I began by drawing certain analogies between the answers to factual 'Why?'-questions and the answers to practical 'Why?'-questions. However, there are disanalogies as well. For instance, there is no inconsistency in saying both 'The fact that your men would be safer is a reason why you should stay' and 'The fact that Cleopatra is leaving is a reason why you should desert.' But it is inconsistent to say both 'The fact that the windows were left open is one reason why the pipes froze' and 'The fact that the heat was turned up was one reason why they didn't freeze.' These two entail both that the pipes froze and that they didn't freeze, whereas the former two do not entail both that Antony should and shouldn't desert. Obviously there can be reasons for doing something at the same time that there are reasons for not doing it. And this shows that although to give both these reasons is to assert both that Cleopatra is leaving and that Antony's men would be safer if he stayed, it is not to prescribe categorically either that he stay or that he go. For to call some consideration, R, merely *a* reason why agent A should do X is not to prescribe that he do it. My suggestion is that it is to say 'Other things being equal, A should do X because of R.' And to say this is neither to say that other things are equal nor to prescribe that, because of R, A should do X.

But to say that a consideration is *the* reason to do something is among other things to prescribe doing what the consideration is said to be the reason to do. To prevent a possible misunderstanding I should emphasize that to call a consideration '*the* reason' in this sense is not to affirm uniqueness. It is not to say that the consideration is the only reason to do whatever it is; this is merely to say that it is *a* reason to do it and there are no other reasons. What is meant is rather that it is a sufficient, conclusive, or overriding reason to do it, and there cannot be sufficient reasons both to do and not to do the same thing. To say that one reason to do X, the fact that P, overrides another reason not to do X, the fact that Q, is to say something like 'Other things being equal, do X because P rather than refrain from X because Q.' Of course, when we call something a sufficient reason we are not suggesting that it is sufficient in all circumstances, but only in those which actually obtain. What happens to be a sufficient reason to do something in one set of circumstances might be overridden by other considerations in different circumstances.

There is a tendency to suppose that one thing cannot provide a reason for another unless there is a relation of logical entailment or quasi-entailment holding between the two. This is certainly a mistake. If we are to make any sense at all of the suggestion that a statement of fact might logically entail a prescription, and thereby provide a logically conclusive reason for doing what is prescribed, I think we must require as at least a necessary condition of there being such an entailment that it be logically impossible not to do what is prescribed when the statement is true. But we normally wish to say that certain facts can provide the reason for doing something, or, if you like, a conclusive and overriding reason for doing it, even when those facts do not make it impossible to avoid doing it. Certainly in the theoretical example, when we say that the reason why the pipes froze is that the windows were left open, we are not asserting that the statement that the windows were left open logically entails the proposition that the pipes froze. It is not *logically* impossible for the windows to be left open and the pipes not to freeze; it is only supposed to be *causally* impossible. In the practical case, there is no sense whatever in which it is impossible not to do what there is a conclusive reason to do; the fact that the soldiers fighting for him would be in serious danger if he abandoned them was just such a reason for Antony to stay, but that didn't stop him from leaving. Of course, if my analysis is correct he could not *think* it was a sufficient reason to stay without intending to stay, but that is another matter altogether. It could nevertheless *be* a conclusive reason for him to stay whether or not he took it to be one.

'THE FACT THAT . . .'

There is, however, a tendency to use the word 'fact' in a very broad sense so that even singular prescriptions turn out to be statements of fact that are either true or false. According to this usage a sentence is capable of expressing a true or false proposition if its grammatical form is such that when it is prefixed by the operator 'the fact that . . .' the result is a noun phrase. Thus, any complete sentence which can be placed after such words as 'Antony wondered whether . . .' or 'Antony asked why . . .', thereby forming another sentence, is also of the right form to appear after the words 'the fact that . . .'. Consequently, if it makes sense to say that Antony wondered whether he should stay behind, even in the sense of 'should' whose sole function is to render into indirect discourse the direct quotation 'Antony wondered "Shall I stay behind?"', then it will also make sense to speak of the fact that he should stay behind, in the same sense of 'should'. But it has never been explained how there could be such things as true prescriptions, any more than there could be true questions. If we consider the prescription we might have addressed to Antony, 'Stay behind with your soldiers', what do we find in it that is capable of truth or falsehood? We might say that it at least presupposes the truth of the proposition that he has some soldiers left to stay behind with, but this is equally presupposed by the contradictory advice 'Don't stay with your soldiers; go after Cleopatra.' It is also presupposed by the question 'Shall I stay behind with my soldiers?', which might be analysed as 'There is some object x, such that x is a soldier of mine; and shall I stay behind with x?.' Obviously this is not what people mean by 'prescriptive fact'.

It is sometimes maintained that prescriptions are disguised reports of the speaker's wishes, so that, for example, my request that you should open the window is really a statement to the effect that I would like you to do it. But this cannot be right, since you can without any inconsistency agree that I would like you to open the window while at the same time refusing to open it. This would not be possible if agreeing that I would like you to open the window were the same as agreeing to open it. But apart from these, I do not know which facts prescriptions have ever been thought to state.

There is a related mistake which it is tempting to make solely because of a misleading feature of surface grammar. Sentences of the form 'The fact that P is a reason for A to do X' do appear to consist of a subject-expression, 'The fact that P', to which is attached a predicate, 'is the reason for A to do X'. And then it can seem that such a sentence has truth-conditions which are satisfied when the entity referred to by the subject-expression has the property or stands in the relation which the predicate is used to ascribe to it. According to this view, the sense of the predicate determines its extension by laying down necessary and sufficient conditions which a fact must meet in order to be a reason for doing a particular thing. Any fact which meets these conditions will be said to 'satisfy' the predicate in the way that an object fits a description. In that case, anyone who agrees that a certain fact has the features which the sense of this predicate lays down will be committed, on pain of violating a conventional rule for the application of the predicate, to agreeing that it is the reason for doing whatever it is. If he does not agree, he will be guilty of inconsistency. But the problem with this view is that it locates the inconsistency in the wrong place. For there is no inconsistency in assenting to a statement of fact and at the same time dissenting from a prescription if it is possible not to do what is prescribed even when the statement is true. So if the fact in question can have those features which are alleged by definition to make it a sufficient reason for A to do X when it is nevertheless possible for A not to do X, then A will not be committed on pain of inconsistency to agreeing to do X once he has agreed that the fact has those features and hence is a conclusive or overrriding reason for doing it. There is surely something odd in saying 'Although the fact that P is a conclusive reason for you to do X, nevertheless don't do it'; my analysis identifies the oddity as an inconsistency.

Now the whole of the foregoing theory was designed to take account of the following data. When someone asks 'shall I do X?' he is not asking whether some fact obtains, and therefore when we answer 'yes' we are not stating a fact. If he then asks 'Why?' he is not asking why any fact obtains, so when we tell him the reason why, we are not saying why some fact obtains. The theory does not readily explain what it means to say 'Antony should *have* stayed with his men'; it also requires anyone who *thinks* that agent A should do X to *intend* that he do it. But anyone who has a different theory will have to accommodate or else challenge the data.

REASONS AND DESIRE

Hume believed that reason was motivationally inert and could not exert on its own any influences on the will. By this he meant that reasoning concerning matters of fact and relations of ideas was incapable by itself of motivating us to do anything, and that factual beliefs required to be supplemented by a 'passion' of some sort if action was to result. To use one of Hare's examples,[1] if I know that before me are both a dish of toadstools which are poisonous and a dish of mushrooms which are not, then something like a desire is required to determine which of them, if either, I will eat. If I wish to die or get very ill my beliefs will motivate me to eat the toadstools, but if I want to say alive I will eat the mushrooms. Reasoning will lead me to certain beliefs about the likely effects of various courses of action and the suitability of different things as means to a given end. But desire is necessary to determine which effect I choose to bring about and which end I choose to promote.

Utility is only a tendency to a certain end; and were the end totally indifferent to us, we should feel the same indifference towards the means. (*Enquiry Concerning the Principles of Morals*, sec. 235)

Hume believed that our innate, if limited, sympathy provided us with a natural impulse to benevolence and that reasoning could direct the impulse to secure its aims but could never give rise to it.

This theory about the relation between factual beliefs and motivation is reformulated by Hare as a theory about the logical relations between statements of fact and prescriptions. In the logic of satisfaction, one prescription entails another only if it is logically impossible to satisfy or fulfil the first without at the same time fulfilling the second. And a statement of fact entails a prescription only if it is logically impossible for the statement to be true without the prescription being satisfied. Since the truth of the statement 'Toadstools are poisonous' obviously does not ensure the satisfaction of the prescription 'Do not eat toadstools', it follows that the statement does not entail the prescription. And consequently one can assent to the former and dissent from the latter without being guilty of any logical inconsistency. But if one already accepts the prescription 'Do not eat what is poisonous' then a belief in the factual statement would logically commit him to refrain from eating toadstools. But if he accepts no prescription which, in conjunction with the statement that toadstools are poisonous, entails a prescription not to eat them, then a belief that they are poisonous will not motivate him to avoid eating them. What is needed to secure motivation is the sort of thing which Hume called an 'impulse' and of which the typical examples are desires. For Hare, they are any mental state whose linguistic expression is some prescription which, together with the factual statement, entails the prescriptive conclusion.

Now it has recently been denied[2] that factual beliefs always require to be supplemented by the presence of an independent desire before they will motivate action. It is not always clear what is meant by an 'independent' desire, but it seems to be one that is not motivated by the same reasons that explain the action. One that is very often cited as an example is the desire to stay dry, which is specified elliptically when we explain a person's taking an umbrella by his belief that it is likely to rain and that if he does not take one he will get wet; in such a case the desire is simply too obvious to need mentioning. But clearly, in the absense of a desire to stay dry, the belief that he will get wet if he does not take an umbrella will not by itself motivate him to take one.

This is contrasted with the case of someone taking steps to ensure that a certain state of affairs will obtain in the future, a case which is alleged to be completely explained by pointing to his belief that doing so will satisfy a future desire of his and which does not require the addition of an independent present desire that this future desires be satisfied. If we do ascribe to him a desire that his future desires be satisfied it is said to be a desire which we have no grounds for suspecting other than the fact that the belief does motivate him. The statement 'He has a present desire to satisfy his future desires' is simply a logical consequence of the statement 'What motivates him to act in the way he does is his belief that acting in that way will satisfy his future desires.' And since having the desire is a logical consequence of being motivated by the belief, it is thought that the desire cannot be an *independent* component (distinct from the belief) in the *explanation* of the action. As McDowell puts it,

> the desire is not a further component, over and above the prudent person's conception of the likely effects of his action on his own future, in the explanation of his behaviour. It is not that the two people share a certain neutral conception of the facts, but differ in that one, but not the other, has an independent desire as well, which combines with that neutral conception of the facts to cast a favourable light on his acting in a certain way. The desire is ascribable to the prudent person simply in recognition of the fact that his conception of the likely effects of his action on his own future by itself casts a favourable light on his acting as he does. ('Are Moral Requirements Hypothetical Imperatives?', p. 16)

But there appears to be a strong objection to the view that the mere belief that acting in a certain way would promote a person's future welfare is sufficient to explain his acting in that way. The difficulty is that two people seem in fact perfectly capable of sharing this belief even though only one of them is motivated to act. For I too may believe that securing a certain result will promote some person's welfare, but if I do not care about his welfare, or if I care more about my own, I will not be motivated by the belief to secure this result for him. How can the ascription of a belief be sufficient on its own to explain why a person acts as he does when not everyone who has the belief acts like that? A defender of the motivational sufficiency of such beliefs must deny that he and I really share the same belief. And of course there is a sense in which it is not true to say 'Each of us believes that bringing about this state of affairs will promote his own welfare' since I do not believe that it will promote *my* welfare. What I believe is that it will promote *his* welfare; and so does he. But the sense in which it is not true to say this is one in which 'his own welfare' does not refer to the welfare of anyone in particular. If it is used to refer to his welfare rather than mine, then the statement is true: *both* of us believe that it will promote his welfare and not mine. The only difference between us seems to be that in his case the person doing the believing and the person which the belief is about are identical. And this is not a difference in what is believed. Whatever it is that determines whose future welfare I care about, whether my own or someone else's, it cannot be simply beliefs; for these are things which many people can share without all being equally concerned for the welfare of the same person.

Turning from prudential to altruistic behaviour, the anti-Humean will follow the same line if we present a case in which two people apparently have the same factual beliefs about their circumstances but one sees no reason to act as the virtuous person would, while the other does. Again it would appear that beliefs on their own cannot suffice to explain their different behaviour since their beliefs seem to be the same. And once more the reply will be to deny that the factual beliefs really are identical and to maintain that the person who sees no reason to act as the virtuous person would cannot really have the same conception of the facts as the virtuous person:

It would be wrong to infer that the conceptions of situations which constitutes the reasons are available equally to people who are not swayed by them, and weigh with those who are swayed only contingently upon their possession of an independent desire . . . we should say that the relevant conceptions are not so much as possessed except by those whose wills are influenced appropriately. (Ibid., p. 23)

This may seem problematic. But if one concedes that a conception of the facts can constitute the whole of a reason for prudent behaviour, one is not at liberty to object to the very idea that a view of how things are might not need supplementing with a desire in order to reveal the favourable light in which someone saw some action; and a view with that property surely cannot be shared by someone who sees no reason to act in the way in question. (Ibid., p. 16)

But as I have just argued, there is no reason to think that prudent behaviour can be explained solely by the agent's belief that his behaviour will satisfy his future desires. If I too believe that securing a certain result would satisfy his future desires, but only he is moved to act by this belief, then he *must* have something I don't have – and it is not a further belief, because I could share that belief and still care more about my own welfare. If he and I were on opposite teams in a championship football game we might both agree that a victory for his team would further his interests just as much as a victory for my team would further mine. And although the beliefs we both share motivate him to score points against my team, they obviously don't motivate *me* to score against my own team. I can see here no relevant belief or conception of the facts that we cannot both share: where we differ is that he prefers that *his* interests be furthered, while I do not; I prefer *my* interests to be furthered.

It will then be objected that it is either empirically false or else trivially true to say that the person who is motivated by beliefs about his future welfare must have a desire to promote his future welfare (since otherwise the beliefs would not have motivated him). It is empirically false if it states that beliefs always require to be backed up by introspectible feelings or tensions before they can motivate action; but if 'desire' is taken to mean just *whatever* it happens to be that enables a belief to motivate action then the claim is obviously true but trivially tautological. For in that sense, to say that a person desires the satisfaction of his future desires is to say nothing more than that he is in fact motivated to act upon the belief that doing so will secure their satisfaction. Thus, to say that beliefs must be accompanied by desire if they are to motivate action is just to say 'Beliefs must be accompanied by whatever it is that enables them to motivate action if they are to motivate action.'

This is indeed tautological, but it is not trivial if whatever it is (we know not what) that enables beliefs to motivate action is something distinct from the beliefs themselves. For the issues is precisely whether this unknown something is an independent component, not whether the presence of some such component follows analytically from the success of beliefs in motivating action. Opium apparently puts some people to sleep. But if it does not put to sleep everyone who takes it then we look for some independent factor to explain why it has the 'soporific power' or 'dormitive virtue' in some cases but not in others. We do not insist that the people who were put to sleep did not really take the same drug as those who were not; we can examine both drugs beforehand and verify as carefully as we please that they are alike in all the relevant respects. Instead, we look for some difference in the constitutions of those who took the opium.

If the inputs are the same but the outputs are different, the proper thing to do is to look for a difference in the internal mechanism which transforms the one into the other. To explain why the outputs differ in the way they do, even though the inputs are identical, it is not enough to say that there must be *some* difference or other in the internal mechanism; we have to devise a theory about precisely *what* the difference is and be able to test this theory otherwise than by simply observing a correlation between input and output. If we can do this we will be able to account for the disposition to fall asleep upon taking opium which is present in some people but not in others. It is certainly tautological to say that if someone had no disposition to fall asleep upon taking opium then he need not have fallen asleep when he took it. What that shows, however, is not that the opium is sufficient to put him to sleep on its own without the presence in him of an independent disposition, but rather than we do not explain anything by calling it simply a disposition.

It is partly true and partly false to say that the disposition does not function as an *independent* component in the *explanation*, needed in order to account for the ability of the opium to put someone to sleep, on the grounds that the existence of the disposition is a logical consequence of the fact that the drug does put him to sleep. What is false is that the disposition is not an independent component which is required if the opium is to have its effect; what is true is that to call the independent component simply a "disposition" is not to explain anything. Clearly his having a disposition to fall asleep upon taking opium is a distinct state of affairs from his actually taking the opium, although we do not explain the power of the drug until we say which physiological states and processes constitute having the disposition. So it is confusion to mix up these quite separate points by saying that a disposition is not a separate component in the explanation: for it *is* a component separate from the input, although to call it just a 'disposition' is not to explain how the input is transformed into an output. Being a separate component is one thing; whether you explain anything by citing it depends entirely on the description under which you cite it. I think the confusion arises because the presence of the disposition is a logical consequence of the success of the input in producing the output, and if it is a mere logical consequence then it cannot explain the output, and if it isn't part of the explanation then it isn't part of the cause. But, as Professor Davidson once remarked,

> there is something very odd in the idea that causal relations are empirical rather than logical. What can this mean? Surely not that every true causal statement is empirical. For suppose 'A caused B' is true. Then the cause of B = A; so substituting, we have 'The cause of B caused B', which is analytic. The truth of a causal statement depends on *what* events are described; its status as analytic or synthetic depends on *how* the events are described. (Donald Davidson: 'Actions, Reasons, and Causes', reprinted in *Essays on Actions and Events*, OUP, 1980, p. 14)

So the argument 'Either empirically false or trivially true' is fallacious as it is used here to refute the Humean view that desire is a disposition distinct from belief and required if belief is to do any motivating. All that is true is that we do not explain anything by referring to this independent component as a 'desire', meaning thereby simply whatever it is that enables belief to motivate action. We have to say exactly what it is before alluding to it will contribute to an explanation of behaviour.

Now although some desires are ascribed to an agent solely as a logical consequence of the fact that certain beliefs motivate him to act, there are other desires for whose presence we can have evidence independently of knowing what his beliefs are. For instance, the desire for drink may be caused by heat, dry air, or dehydration and may exist whether or not the thirsty person has any beliefs about how to procure something to drink. In this case our grounds for attributing to him a desire to drink are *not* based solely, or even at all, upon noticing how his belief that acting in a certain way will get him something to drink motivates him to act in precisely that way. If he is a slave toiling in the hot sun we can see by his perspiration that he is thirsty even though he has no opportunity to take steps to satisfy his thirst.

Let us contrast this 'unmotivated' desire for something to drink with Professor Nagel's example of a 'motivated' desire to do something in particular as a means to satisfying this desire.

If I am thirsty and a soft-drink machine is available, I shall feed it a dime, open the resulting bottle, and drink. In such a case desire, belief, and rudimentary theoretical reasoning evidently combine somehow to produce action. . . . Upon reflection, it can seem mysterious that *thirst* should be capable of motivating someone not just to drink, but to put a dime in a slot. . . . It is of course true that when one sees that the only way to get a drink is to put a dime in the slot, one then wants to put a dime in the slot. But that is what requires explanation; . . . For example, it is imaginable that thirst should cause me to want to put a dime in my pencil sharpener . . . (*The Possibility of Altruism*, pp. 33–4)

It is certainly right to deny that for this motivation to occur it should be necessary that there already be in his repository of desires a standing desire to go around feeding money to vending machines. He is not out of luck if, before he notices the possibility of getting satisfaction from the machine, he does not happen to have an independent inclination to put money into soft-drink machines anyway. His thirst together with his belief about the machine will themselves give rise to this desire. But how? Why doesn't it give rise to a desire to put a dime in the pencil sharpener?

I think the explanation begins with the observation that part of wanting to satisfy one's thirst is wanting to take the most appropriate steps in the circumstances to satisfy it. Expressing this in terms of assent to various prescriptions, we may say that anyone who wants to get something to drink is in a mental state whose expression in language is 'Let me get something to drink'. And this entails the prescription 'Let me take the most appropriate steps in the circumstances to get something to drink'. If we add the further premise expressed by the sentence 'Putting money into the machine is the most appropriate step under the circumstances to getting something to drink' we have a pair of premises which logically entail the prescriptive conclusion 'Let me put money into the machine' and not, for instance, 'Let me put money into the pencil sharpener.' It may be objected that the further premise is not entirely factual since it says not only that putting money into the machine is *a* means of getting something to drink; it says that it is the *best* means. But this does not affect my argument in any way. Nagel requires an explanation for the appropriateness of the desire to feed money to the soft-drink machine rather than to the pencil sharpener, given the desire for drink and the belief about the machine. My answer is that to have the desire and the belief is to assent to a certain prescription and a certain proposition, where the items assented to themselves entail the prescription 'Let me put money into the machine'. And sincere assent to this prescription is part of wanting to put money into the machine. That is why this desire is appropriate.

Now although the two premisses entail the prescriptive conclusion, assent to the premisses does not by itself entail assent to the conclusion. But this is not surprising. From the fact that some set of factual premisses entails a certain factual conclusion, it does not follow that if someone believes the premisses he will also believe the conclusion: he might not see the entailment until he is shown the steps of the proof, and only then believe the conclusion. In some cases it is difficult to imagine how someone could accept the premisses and not the conclusion; e.g. how someone could believe that A is greater than B, and that B is greater than C, and yet not believe A is greater than C. Nevertheless, believing the conclusion is something different from believing the premisses; and although the premisses entail the conclusion, sincere assent to the premisses does not *entail* sincere assent to the conclusion – it only *commits* one on pain of inconsistency not to deny the conclusion. The same holds of inferences involving prescriptions. The desire which consists in sincere assent to the prescription 'Let me put money into the soft-drink machine' is distinct from the states of mind whose linguistic expressions are 'Let me procure something to drink' and 'Putting money into the machine is the best way to get something to drink.' And although *what is said* in uttering (1) 'Let me adopt the most appropriate means to getting something to drink' and (2) 'Putting money in the machine is the most appropriate means to getting something to drink' logically entails the prescription expressed by (3) 'Let me put money into the machine', nevertheless sincere assent to (1) and (2) does not by itself entail sincere assent to (3); and therefore having the desire and belief represented by (1) and (2) does not entail having the desire to put money into the machine. I am unable to explain why the desire and belief represented by (1) and (2) give rise to the desire represented by (3), just as I am unable to explain why believing that A is larger than B and that B is larger than C causes one to believe that A is larger than C. But that does not make me doubt that the desire represented by (3) is distinct from the states of mind expressed by (1) and (2) any more than it makes me doubt that the belief that A is larger than C is distinct from the belief that A is larger than B and B is larger than C.

SEEING A FACT AS CONSTITUTING A REASON TO DO SOMETHING

Imagine a case in which two people believe that a certain person, say Jones, is lonely, depressed, and wants someone to talk to.[3] One of them sees this as a reason to engage Jones in conversation, while the other does not. Rather, he sees it as a reason to avoid Jones altogether. McDowell resists any interpretation of this situation according to which both people share a neutral conception of the facts but take these facts to provide reasons for doing different things because they have different dispositions. He insists that they do not even have the same conception of the facts, and that what he calls the 'virtuous person's' conception is only available to someone who takes the facts as a reason to talk to Jones.

It might seem that we can determine empirically whether McDowell is right by asking each of the persons to state his conception of the relevant facts. But even if they state the same facts in the same words, this will not convince him that their conception of those facts is the same. The closest analogy is perhaps provided by those drawings which can be seen in either of two ways: the cube which seems at one moment to be viewed from above and the next moment from below, or the silhouette which can be seen either as a goblet or as two faces looking at each other. If the people who see these drawings in different ways were asked to copy what they see onto separate sheets of paper, the resultant drawings might be indistinguishable to such an extent that no one was later able to identify which was his. They may all look at the same original, reproduce the same features, and yet still see it in different ways. And this means perhaps that the copies they produce are inadequate expressions of how they see the original. Similarly, McDowell might concede that two people could describe the same features of Jones' situation in the same words, and yet somehow conceive of the situation differently. This would mean simply that their linguistic behaviour was an inadequate expression of the way they saw the situation.

Clearly it is going to be difficult to tell whether they 'conceive' of the situation in the same way independently of observing what they take the situation as providing a reason to do. In fact, on McDowell's view this turns out to be logically impossible:

Conveying what a circumstance means, in this loaded sense, is getting someone to see it in the special way in which a virtuous person would see it [viz.] to see situations in a special light, as constituting reasons for acting. ('Are Moral Requirements Hypothetical Imperatives?', p. 21)

He says that we 'see' the features of a situation as providing reasons to act in a certain way by the exercise of a perceptual capacity which makes us sensitive to the moral requirements imposed by circumstances:

> That the situation requires a certain sort of behaviour is (one way of formulating) his reason for behaving in that way, on each of the relevant occasions. So it must be something of which, on each of the relevant occasions, he is aware. A kind person has a reliable sensitivity to a certain sort of requirement which situations impose on behaviour. The deliverances of a reliable sensitivity are cases of knowledge; and there are idioms according to which the sensitivity itself can appropriately be described as knowledge: a kind person knows what it is like to be confronted with a requirement of kindness. The sensitivity is, we might say, a sort of perceptual capacity. ('Virtue and Reason', pp. 331–2)

But this notion of a perceptual capacity that makes us sensitive to moral requirements (presumably in the way that our visual capacity makes us sensitive to light) is open to precisely the objections which Professor Strawson urged against old-fashioned ethical Intuitionism.[4] For let us suppose that it is a *fact* about a situation that it requires a certain sort of behaviour. At the very least this fact will be supervenient upon some ordinary empirical facts of the situation; e.g. the situation requires of me that I engage Jones in conversation *because* he is lonely, depressed, and wants a friend to talk to, and I am his friend (where being his friend is again supervenient upon the fact that I bear to him a certain empirically describable relation). Now either the requirement of the situation is identical with the empirical facts upon which it is supervenient (in which case we need no special perceptual capacity, since awareness of the empirical facts is the same as awareness of the requirement), or it is distinct from them (in which case awareness of the requirement must be distinct from awareness of the empirical facts, in which case it must be possible to be aware of the requirement independently of being aware of any of the empirical facts of the situation which impose the requirement, which is absurd).

It will not do to suggest that, although the requirement is identical with the empirical facts, awareness of the requirement is awareness of the facts under a different description, so that one could be aware of the facts as described in one way without being aware of the requirement as described in some other way. For either it is an empirical description or it isn't: if it is, then we don't need any sixth sense to determine whether it applies; and if it isn't, then we must be able to determine whether it applies independently of knowing any of the facts in virtue of which it applies.

We can avoid the quicksands of Intuitionism by realizing that to regard certain features of a situation as constituting a reason to behave in a certain way is not to believe any fact about those features: it is just to give sincere assent to the prescription to act in that way, other things being equal, because of those features. Now since sincere assent to the prescription that an action be done is nothing else than the intention that the action be done, it follows that McDowell is right in saying that the conception of the situation as providing a reason to do something is 'not so much as possessed except by those whose wills are influenced appropriately'. But such a conception is not a factual belief about the situation.

So the attempt to show that factual beliefs may be sufficient all by themselves to motivate action cannot proceed by arguing that someone who conceives of a situation as constituting a reason to act in a certain way is *thereby* motivated in a certain degree to act in that way. It is trivially true that the agent must have a *disposition* to act when he acquires a factual belief or else the belief would not motivate him to act. It is not, however, a trivial question whether this disposition has an underlying basis which accounts for it or rather is an ultimate, brute, and inexplicable fact. It might be true that if a train had come down a particular track it would have ended up on siding #1 instead of siding #2, and so we could say that there are circumstances in which trains which go down that track have a disposition to end up on siding #1. This disposition has an underlying basis: the fact that the switch was left in a certain position by the flagman. Newton's Law of Universal Gravitation states that every particle in the universe attracts every other particle with a force directly proportional to the product of their masses and inversely proportional to the square of the distance between them. Some people maintain that this is an ultimate law, that there is no reason whatever why objects are disposed to accelerate towards each other at a rate inversely proportional to the square and not the *cube* of the distance. As I understand it, the claim that factual beliefs can motivate action all by themselves amounts to the assertion that the disposition to act upon acquiring a belief is one which, like inertia and gravitation, has no underlying basis; I, however, hold out hope that it is not ultimate and that there is something yet to be discovered which explains it.

JUSTIFICATION AND MOTIVATION

Let me again stipulate how I intend to use the words 'explanation' and 'justification'. Considering first a factual question of the form 'Is it the case that P?' we can see that any affirmative or negative answer must be either true or false; to give any such answer is to state that some fact obtains. If it is then asked 'Why is it the case that P?' we can only answer by saying something of the form 'It is the case that P *because* it is the case that Q.' Now if Q's being the case really is why P is the case, then I say it is the explanation of P's being the case. And consequently, to explain, in this sense, is always to say why some fact obtains. On the other hand, if we consider a practical question of the form 'Shall I do X?' we can see than an affirmative or negative answer can be neither true nor false; to give any such answer is to prescribe that X be done. Suppose the answer is 'No, do not do X'; if I then ask 'Why not?', thereby asking why I should not do X, I am not asking why any fact obtains since the negative answer I received did not tell me that any fact obtained. My 'Why?'-question can only be answered by saying something of the form 'Do not do X *because* it is the case that Q', thereby saying why I should not do X. If Q's being the case really is why I should not do X, then I say it is the justification of my not doing X. So in this sense, to justify is never to say why some fact obtains. Now to ask what motivated someone to perform a certain action is to ask for an *explanation* of why it is the case that he did it. It is not to ask for any kind of justification of his action. It may be true or false that Q's being the case is what motivated his action, but it can never be true or false that Q's being the case is what justifies his action – at least in the sense of 'justify' which I have just expounded. I am not claiming that the words 'explain' and 'justify' are normally used exactly as I have stipulated; I am merely attempting to draw a distinction between answering a factual 'Why?'-question and answering a practical 'Why?'-question, and using these words to mark that distinction.

With this in mind, let us examine Professor Nagel's criticism of Hume's theory of motivation.

The position I am attacking explains prudential conduct by saying that my future interests give me reasons to act because I have a present desire to further those interests. On this view future desires cannot by themselves provide reasons, but present desires can. (*The Possibility of Altruism*, p. 39)

What is being attacked is a theory which explains how action is motivated, a theory according to which the belief that I will have certain desires in the future cannot by itself motivate me to ensure the satisfaction of those desires; it needs to be supplemented by a present desire that my future desires be satisfied. This theory must not be mistaken for a quite different view which holds that statements about future desires can never by themselves provide justification for pursuing a certain course of action, i.e. *reason to* pursue it. The latter view need not be maintained by anyone who adopts the former. The difference may be brought out clearly by pointing out that according the view Nagel proposes to attack a question of the form 'Why is A doing X?' is not completely answered by saying 'because A believes that in the future he will desire the occurence of the state of affairs resulting from X'; for someone else may also believe that A will desire that state of affairs to be brought about and yet not be motivated to do X because he does not wish A's future desire to be satisfied. But according to the other view, with which Hume's is in danger of being confused, a question of the form 'Why do X?' can never be adequately answered by saying 'because you will in future desire the occurence of the state of affairs resulting from X'.

There is no reason to believe this other view to be true. We often quite properly advise people to do things and back up our advice by pointing solely to their future desires. If they do not happen to desire the satisfaction of those desires then they will not be motivated merely by accepting the factual considerations we adduce. But we do not have to stop thinking that those considerations really are the reasons why they should act as we advise (where to say that they *should* act in that way is not to state a fact). *Their* refusal to regard the question 'Why do X?' as being satisfactorily answered by the reason 'because Y' is no reason for *us* to stop assenting to the prescription 'Do X because Y.'

Nagel attempts to render implausible the theory he is attacking by drawing from it apparent consequences which seem paradoxical. He tries to imagine what might happen if the desire for the satisfaction of some known future desires were absent, or if there were a present

desire for some future state of affairs which it was known would not
be desired at the future time.

> First, given that any desire with a future object provides a basis of
> reasons to do what will promote that object, it may happen that I
> now desire for the future something which I shall not and do not
> expect to desire then, and which I believe there will then be no
> reason to bring about. Consequently I may have reason now to
> prepare to do what I know I will have no reason to do when the
> time comes. (Ibid., p. 39)

This passage owes whatever force it has to the fact that we are not
sure what sort of reasons are being alluded to. If the reasons are
supposed to be of the explanatory sort then the passage is correct but
the consequence it mentions is in no way paradoxical; and if the
reasons are of the justificatory sort then what he says is not true. The
theory he is attacking does hold that any desire with a future object
provides a basis of motivation to do what will promote that object.
The theory does not necessarily hold that a present desire provides
any justification for promoting the future object of that desire.
Someone who wishes to pour gasoline on his pet cat tomorrow and
set it on fire may indeed be motivated to buy gasoline today, but
there is no need to think he is justified in doing so. The correct
answer to the factual question 'Why is he buying gasoline today?'
may be the explanatory reason 'because he wants to burn alive his cat
tomorrow'. But this does not entail that an equally satisfactory
answer to the practical question 'Why buy gasoline today?' is provided by the justificatory reason 'because I want to burn alive my cat
tomorrow'. One could appropriately reply that since there is no good
reason to burn his cat, there is no good reason to buy gasoline to burn
it with. The fact that *he* thinks his desire to burn his cat is a good
reason to buy gasoline does not commit *us* to thinking it is a good
reason.

If I desire to bring about something in the future, and know that at
the future date I will not want it brought about, in what sense do I
believe, as Nagel says, that there will be no reason to bring it about?
Suppose that today I desire to have my house air-conditioned tomorrow but know that tomorrow I shall have had time to be persuaded
against it by thoughts of the money it will cost me. Tomorrow I will
not *see* the summer heat as a good enough reason to spend large sums
on air-conditioning, and in that sense I will not be *motivated* to do so.

But from this it does not follow that tomorrow the same summer heat will not *be* good enough reason to spend that much money, in the sense that I will no longer be *justified* in doing so. I know that tomorrow I will think the expense is too much and will cancel the order for installation; but I also know that if I live with the air-conditioning for a few days I will come to think that the money was well spent. So in what sense would I 'have reason now to prepare to do what I know I will have no reason to do when the time comes?'. It is true that I may be motivated now to do what I know I will lack motivation to do when the time comes. But perhaps I should make sure that I am out of harm's way tomorrow so that my lack of motivation then will not interfere with what I am motivated to do now.

That was an example in which a present desire for a future state of affairs was known to be accompanied by the absence at the relevant future time of any desire for that state of affairs. The situation is reversed in the next case; a present lack of desire for a future object is known to be followed by a future desire at the appropriate time for the same object.

> Suppose that I expect to be assailed by a desire in the future: then I must acknowledge that in the future I will have prima facie reason to do what the desire indicates. But this reason does not obtain now, and cannot by itself apply derivatively to any presently available means to the satisfaction of the future desire. Thus in the absence of any further relevant desire in the present, I may have no reason to prepare for what I know I shall have reason to do tomorrow. (Ibid., p. 40)

This apparent paradox can be disarmed just like the last one by observing the distinction between motivation and justification. If I expect to have some desire in the future then I must acknowledge that in the future I will have some *motivation* to do what the desire indicates, but I need not acknowledge that I will have even prima facie *justification* for doing it. There is nothing in the least paradoxical in the fact that I may *not* be motivated today to prepare for what I know I will be motivated to do tomorrow. This will occur whenever I am motivated to prevent the realization of the object of the future desire more than I am motivated to prevent the frustration arising from that unsatisfied desire: the standard example is Odysseus who has himself tied to the mast so that he is unable to yield to the lure of the sirens.

Nagel does consider the case of an expected future desire whose satisfaction conflicts with that of a current desire, and tries to argue that according to Hume's theory it would be possible in such a case to have no *reason* now to do something which I know I will have reason in the future to have done. But the following explanatory comment reveals how the force of this charge rests entirely on a confusion of motivation with justification.

> This must not be confused with the perfectly unobjectionable and not uncommon case in which someone puts obstacles in his way knowing that he will *want* something in the future which he should not have. This may induce him to put a time lock on the liquor cabinet, for example. But that is because he expects to want to do what he will at that time have reason *not* to do. . . . One does not have reason now to ensure the frustration of what it will be *rational* to do in the future. (Ibid., p. 40, n. 1)

Nagel admits that it is possible for someone to know that he will be motivated to have something which he knows (or at least believes) he will not be justified in having. And if someone will not be justified in having a thing tomorrow, then he may be justified today in taking steps to ensure that he does not get it tomorrow. So there may well be present justification for ensuring the impossibility of what there will be future *motivation* to do. What Nagel is apparently denying is that there could be present justification for arranging the frustration of what there will be future *justification* to do. But the theory he is supposed to be attacking, which is a theory of motivation, does not have this consequence, and therefore his argument is beside the point.

REASONS AND RELATIVISM

What makes some people tempted to attack Hume's theory of motivation seems to me to be a confusion about how to interpret the perfectly acceptable claim: 'The possession by an agent of a desire need not be part of a reason for him to act in a certain way.' This confusion is dispelled once a distinction is observed between motivating an action and justifying it; for although the agent's possession of a desire is not necessary in order that some course of action on his part be justified, it is necessary if he is to be motivated to take it. Sometimes it is claimed that a consideration cannot provide a reason for someone to act in a certain way unless it reveals to the agent that so acting tends to bring about something he wants. This is not true. If someone were to ask me 'Why not stick pins into the cat just for fun?' I might reply '. . . because you would not like it if pins were stuck into you just for fun'. A sadist would be unlikely to accept this as a reason not to torture the cat, but that does not commit *me* to giving up the claim that it is a reason; it does not even prevent it from *being* a reason. Whether you convince someone to adopt a course of action by citing a particular fact does depend on what his desires are, but whether that fact is a reason why he should adopt it has nothing whatever to do with whether he or anyone else is convinced by that reason to act accordingly. If I were in a position of authority I might order him not to torture the cat, saying 'You shall not stick pins into the cat; that's an order'. This command can be reported in indirect discourse by saying 'I ordered that he should not stick pins into the cat', and my order was a sincere prescription if I thought that he should not do it, and therefore intended that he should not. Again, 'should' is here used simply as the form which 'shall' takes in indirect speech. And in this sense, the question why he should not do it is one to which I still accept the same answer: '. . . because he would not like it done to him'.

My reason for commanding him is something altogether different; he was unlikely to be motivated by anything but the threat of punishment. If he asks again why he should not torture the cat, I would say '. . . because I will punish you if you do', thereby giving him, in my view, *another* reason why he should not, although in his view it is the *only* reason I have given him. But why should the fact that *he thinks* it is the only reason I have given him logically entail that *it is* the only reason I have given him?

Gilbert Harman has maintained that a fact can provide a person with a reason to do something only if that person accepts principles from which, together with that fact, it can be derived that he (at least prima facie) ought to do it.[5] Suppose that a person P does not accept any principle which, together with that fact, entails that he ought to do some action D. Then

P has no reason to do D, at least none that derives from his principles. It is part of our ordinary view that P ought to do D only in cases in which P has reasons to do D. And, it is unclear where those reasons might come from, except from P's principles. For how can *your* principles give P any reason to do D if P does not share your principles? (*The Nature of Morality*, p. 84)

In Professor Harman's illustration, you are a vegetarian while P is not, so you accept principles which forbid the eating of meat but P does not.

Of course, if P had accepted your general principle, the fact that steak is meat would give him a reason not to eat it. But, since he does not accept your principle, how can you suppose that this fact does after all give him such a reason? Surely, you can suppose that this gives him a reason only if you think that P ought to accept your principle rather than his own. So you must think that P has a reason to accept your principle. . . . But if P has no reason to accept your principle or a principle similar to it, it is not clear in what sense the fact that steak is meat could provide him with a reason not to eat steak. (Ibid., p. 88)

It is true that unless a person accepts appropriate principles his awareness of certain facts will not provide him with a *motive* to do anything, and he will not be committed to *acknowledging* that those facts are a reason for him to do anything. In that sense he does not *have* a reason. But it does not follow that there *is* no reason. The ultimate principles which I accept commit me to taking certain facts as a reason to do something; he does not accept those principles and I cannot offer him any further reasons to accept them (or else they would not be ultimate). Thus a consistent carnivore accepts no principle which commits him to agreeing that the fact that steak is meat is a reason why he should not eat it, which is to say that he accepts no principle that entails the first-person prescription 'Other things being equal, I shall not eat steak because it is meat.' But I still accept the second-person prescription which I might have addressed to him earlier: 'Other things being equal, do not eat steak because it is meat.' In other words, I continue to think that the fact that steak is meat is a reason why he should not eat it, and the fact that *he* doesn't accept any reason to think so is irrelevant.

If it is objected that there is no reason why he should think that steak's being meat is a reason not to eat it, I will reply that there is indeed a reason and I will point to my ultimate principle. This principle might be something like 'Always act so that you can wish the maxim of your action were adopted by all rational beings'; but it doesn't really matter what the principle is, so let me abbreviate it by the formula 'Always act in manner M.' I will then say that the reason why steak's being meat is a reason why he should not eat it is that he should always act in manner M. But he doesn't agree that he should act in manner M, and by holding this principle to be ultimate I am admitting that there is no further reason why he (or I, for that matter) should accept it. But that does not show that he is not mistaken in not accepting it; rather it shows that at this level there can be only one respect in which he is mistaken (if indeed he is mistaken at all), namely that although he *should* always act in manner M, yet he *thinks* otherwise. It is not because *I accept* the principle 'Always act in manner M' that he is mistaken to deny that he should act in that manner; it is just because he *should* act in manner M that he is mistaken to deny it. There need not and cannot be any fact by virtue of which he is mistaken to deny this prescription; for this is rock bottom. If there were a fact in virtue of which he should act in manner M, then the principle 'Always act in manner M because of fact F' would itself be the ultimate principle, contrary to the assumption that the ultimate principle was 'Always act in manner M.'

EVIDENCE

To say that certain facts constitute *evidence* in support of a conclusion is to say that they provide *reason to believe* the conclusion. And some reasons for believing a conclusion are better than others. Plato points out (*Gorgias*, 454d) that we quite naturally wish to evaluate true beliefs according to whether or not they amount to knowledge. We think there is a difference between education and indoctrination, instruction and persuasion. Since those who have learned and those who merely believe correctly have both been persuaded, there must be two types of persuasion – one which results in true belief without knowledge and the other which results in knowledge. Rhetoric was criticised on the grounds that the conviction it produced in the courts about right and wrong constituted persuasion but not knowledge. The distinction seems to rest on the quality of the reasons which produce and maintain the belief. And in this there is a clear parallel with morality. Just as we do not account someone moral who does the right thing for the wrong reasons, so he who believes what is true, although for the wrong reasons, is not said to know what he believes.

But to call a consideration a reason to believe something is not to describe the consideration; it is to say something like 'Other things being equal, believe this because . . .', where the blank is filled in with a statement of the fact said to be the reason. We must say 'other things being equal' since, although the consideration in question may be a reason to believe something, there may be other considerations which are better reasons not to believe it. One of the functions of 'because' in a sentence of the form 'Believe that P, because Q' is to introduce a certain element of universalizability; we are saying 'The present circumstances are such that whenever it is true that Q, believe that P; and it *is* the case that Q.' It is of course left unspecified what the present circumstances are, but this is no different from our treatment of ordinary causal statements. If I say 'The pipes froze because the windows were left open' I am implying that there is some universal law that connects open windows and frozen pipes. The law is obviously not 'Whenever the windows are left open the pipes will freeze' since the pipes will not freeze if it is warm outside. All we are implying is that the circumstances at the time were such that whenever the windows are left open in those circumstances the pipes will freeze; and we may not know precisely which of the circumstances obtaining at the time were the relevant ones.

It might seem that on this prescriptivist theory of what it is to call a consideration a reason to believe something, no consideration could be 'really' or 'objectively' a better or worse reason than any other. This would be a mistake. Comparative judgements of the strengths of different reasons can be expressed as follows: to say 'The fact that P is a better reason to believe that Q, than the fact that R is to believe that – Q' is to say 'Other things being equal, believe that Q because of the fact that P, rather than believe – Q because of the fact that R.' To say that all considerations are equally good as reasons is itself to express an evaluation: it is to prescribe that conviction not rest more strongly on some beliefs than on any others. And as a prescription it cannot be anything to which the theory is logically committed. It is certainly open to a prescriptivist to think that it is a better reason for believing the defendent to be innocent that he was a thousand miles from the scene of the crime when it was committed than that he is the nephew of the prime minister. To say that one is no better than the other is to say that there are both equally good (or bad); and this is an evaluation which simply cannot follow from the theory that to call one consideration a better reason than another is to prescribe that we be more firmly convinced by the one than the other.

What a person is willing to call evidence are those considerations which have a tendency to convince him. This is not to say that when a person calls something evidence he is merely stating the ('subjective') fact that he tends to be convinced by it; for he is not stating any fact about the evidence at all. Such a confusion is very easy to make. In Chapter 6 of *Leviathan* Hobbes wrote: 'whatsoever is the object of any man's Appetite or Desire; that is it, which he for his part calleth *Good*: And the object of his Hate, and Aversion, *Evill*'. Professor Raphael's comment on this passage is as follows:

> Hobbes then proceeds in this chapter to give definitions of the terms 'good' and 'evil'. They are defined as the *object* of desire and of aversion respectively. If I call a thing good, according to Hobbes this means that I want it; and if I call a thing bad, this means that I dislike it. (D. D. Raphael, *Hobbes: Morals and Politics*, Allen & Unwin, 1977, p. 42)

It seems that Raphael is saying that, according to Hobbes, if I call something good, what I mean is that I want it; and that if I call a thing bad, what I am saying is that I dislike it. If this is in fact how Raphael is interpreting Hobbes, then the passage from *Leviathan* which he is referring to does not by itself support this interpretation. Hobbes is saying that the things a person calls good and things he wants are always the same things. And this may be because to think something to be good is the same as to want it; but it does not follow that to say that something is good is the same as saying that you want it. Suppose it is true that to say-in-one's-heart an imperative is to have a desire; it does not follow that to say-aloud-with-one's-mouth the same imperative is to *state* that you have a desire, for it is not to state any fact at all.

So the prescriptivist theory of evidence-claims must not be confused with what is called the 'subjective theory of probability'. The subjective theory maintains that a person who says that a particular piece of evidence confers a certain degree of probability on a statement is really just making a psychological report about himself; he is reporting that his awareness of the evidence has aroused in him a certain degree of confidence in the truth of the statement.

In that respect the theory is similar to other subjectivist theories regarding value judgements, for instance the theory that 'This is a good picture' means simply 'I like this picture' and that 'Capital punishment is wrong' means just 'I disapprove of capital punishment.' And in that respect it suffers their defects. For, any theory which holds that 'The fact that P is true makes it very probable that Q is true' means the same as 'My knowledge that P is true makes me very confident that Q is true', or any other such psychological report, will fall victim to G. E. Moore's conclusive refutation in Chapter 3 of his book *Ethics*. If A says 'The truth of P makes it very probable that Q is true' and B says 'The truth of P does not make it very probable that Q is true', then it is a consequence of the subjectivist theory that they are not contradicting each other since it is perfectly possible for what they both say to be true. For, the theory maintains that A is only saying that his knowledge that P is true makes him very confident that Q is true, while B is saying that his knowledge of the truth of P does not make him very confident in the truth of Q; and it is certainly possible for A to be confident while B is not. But it is an obvious linguistic fact that we do not use the word 'probable' in this way; we use it in such a way that the assertions of A and B *are* inconsistent.

Moore used this argument to show that 'X is right' does not mean the same as any such psychological report as 'I approve of X'. For if it did, then when A said 'X is right' and B said 'X is not right' they would *not* be disagreeing with each other; A would only be saying that he approved of X while B would be saying that he did not. But, said Moore, it is an obvious fact that the word 'right' is not used in this way; it is used in such a way that 'X is right' said by A and 'X is not right' said by B express logically inconsistent judgements about the same thing, and that if A and B are sincere in their utterances then they are disagreeing with each other.

C. L. Stevenson, in his reply to Moore,[6] argued that this was not as obvious a fact as Moore had made it out to be. Since there need be no *fact* in dispute when A says 'X is right' and B says 'X is not right', he concluded that A and B need only be 'disagreeing in attitude' and not 'disagreeing in opinion'; and if their disagreement amounts only to a difference of attitude and not a difference of opinion then they are not contradicting each other (p. 83).

This criticism prompted Moore to make a retraction which was at once illuminating and not altogether necessary:

if one member of a party, A, says 'Let's play poker', and another,
B, says 'No, let's listen to a record', A and B can be quite properly
said to be disagreeing . . . when I wrote the *Ethics*, it simply had
not occurred to me that in the case of our two men, who assert
sincerely, in a 'typically ethical' sense of 'right', and both in the
same sense, the one that Brutus' action was right, the other that it
was not, the disagreement between them might possible be merely
of that sort . . . I even go further, I feel some inclination to think
that those two men are *not* making incompatible assertions: that
their disagreement *is* merely a disagreement in attitude. ('A Reply
to My Critics' in Schilpp (ed.), *The Philosophy of G. E. Moore*,
p. 546.)

What is illuminating about Moore's retraction is the example he
offers. If A says 'Let's play poker' and B says 'No, let's listen to a
record', then they are certainly not making incompatible statements
of fact since they are not stating any facts at all. But they are making
incompatible suggestions. And if B had said 'No, let's not play poker'
then their prescriptions would in fact have been *contradictory*; for, it
would be logically impossible for both prescriptions to be satisfied.
What is unnecessary about Moore's retraction is that his very example shows that, even if the disagreement between A and B is merely
one of attitude, what the one says in expressing his attitude can be
logically inconsistent with what the other says in expressing his.
  So Moore's refutation of subjectivism was conclusive after all:
value judgements are not simply reports of the speaker's own psychological states. And the same argument shows that statements of
probability are not just reports of the speaker's subjective degree
of confidence or strength of belief. It is closer to the truth about most
ordinary uses of 'probable' to say that probability statements are
prescriptions to adopt attitudes of confidence and expectancy, instead
of *reports* about actually adopted attitudes. When we say that a piece
of evidence confers a certain degree of probability on a conclusion we
are not reporting any fact at all about the evidence if what we are
saying is that the evidence constitutes a reason to hold a corresponding degree of confidence in the conclusion. For then we are issuing
the prescription: 'Other things being equal, in these circumstances
and because of that evidence, hold this degree of confidence in the
conclusion.' When two people disagree about the strength of the
evidence they are not disagreeing over any *fact* about the evidence;

they disagree over how confident *to be* in the truth of the conclusion, given the evidence.

It can easily strike one as strange that there should even be such things as imperatives prescribing that we believe something. To assent sincerely to a prescription is to intend to do what is prescribed. But how can I intend to believe something which I don't already believe? I can intend to go for a walk in the park tomorrow even though I am not going for a walk in the park now; but it seems nonsensical to suggest that I could intend to believe tomorrow that Napoleon died in 1822 even though I don't believe it now. And yet we certainly do say in the imperative mood such things as 'Don't believe everything you read' and 'Expect me home at 6 o'clock.'

The explanation of these facts concerns the notion of forming an intention. Take a simple example: the office staff are going to lunch together but one of us must stay behind to answer the telephone in case an important client calls, and I am chosen. If I agree to the request and give sincere assent to the prescription 'Stay behind and answer the telephone whenever it rings' then I form the intention to do what I have agreed to do. But intending is not itself a kind of activity. To intend to answer the telephone is not really to *do* anything; it is to be in a dispositional state. And consequently to *form* an intention is not to do anything either; it is to *acquire* a disposition. I may take steps to put myself in such a state, but in that case going into a dispositional state is a *result* of the things that I do and is not itself one of the things that I do. Sleeping, for instance, is not an activity and falling asleep is not an action, but taking sleeping pills is an action that will result in falling asleep. Suppose that I am at first reluctant to stay behind while everyone else has a good time, but that I am eventually persuaded. To persuade me to stay and answer the telephone is to do something which *causes* me to acquire the disposition to stay and answer the telephone. Of course, not just anything that results in my acquiring this disposition will count as persuasion, although I am not sure where to draw the line; perhaps subliminal advertising, if successful, would count as 'hidden' persuasion while putting a drug in my tea would not. At any rate, causing me to acquire a disposition is at least a necessary condition of persuading me to do something.

Intending to believe something is in many respects like intending to do something. If I have been persuaded *that* whatever my teacher says is true then I have been persuaded *to* believe whatever my teacher says; I have acquired a disposition to believe a proposition if my teacher asserts it. All that prevents me from being persuaded today to believe something tomorrow is my inability to acquire the relevant intention. For this intention would have to be a disposition which became activated and precipitated belief under very peculiar circumstances, e.g. my knowing what day it was. If I am persuaded on Tuesday to go for a walk in the park on Wednesday then I have acquired a disposition which will become activated merely by an awareness of what day it is; I have been put into such a state that a realization that today is Wednesday will get me to go for a walk in the park. But I cannot be put into such a state that the mere realization that today is Wednesday would get me to believe something I didn't believe on Tuesday. And yet it is only a contingent fact that I cannot be put into such a state. Almost any consideration might have been capable of persuading me to believe something; but if I have not been convinced by only certain considerations I probably would not have lasted very long in the world.

> Here, then is a kind of pre-established harmony between the course of nature and the succession of our ideas: . . . Those, who delight in the discovery and contemplation of *final causes,* here have ample subject to employ their wonder and admiration.
> I shall add . . . that, as this operation of the mind is so essential to the subsistence of all human creatures, it is . . . more conformable to the ordinary wisdom of nature to secure so necessary an act of the mind by some instinct or mechanical tendency . . . which carries forward the thought in a correspondent course to that which she has established among external objects. (David Hume, *An Enquiry Concerning Human Understanding*, Sec. V, Pt. II.)

Even if the rationality of inductive inferences were a *fact* about them (which it isn't), their mere rationality could not explain why we find them so compelling; we also require an explanation for the fact that our minds are so formed that we are compelled by those inferences and not by others. The fact that $7 + 5 = 12$ does not by itself explain why a pocket calculator displays the numeral '12' when you punch the keys '7', '+', '5', and '='; it is only because of the way in which the internal circuitry is designed that it displays that numeral rather than some other (an obvious case of pre-established harmony).[7]

So the notion of being persuaded to believe is no more mysterious than the notion of being persuaded to act: in both cases persuasion is a *causal* process whose result is the acquisition of a dispositional state. What you can be persuaded to do or believe depends entirely on which dispositions you are capable of acquiring under given circumstances. Some people will sell their grandmothers for $1000, others for only $100, and others not at all; some people will believe in the Resurrection when they hear of the empty sepulchre, others only when they see the spike-holes in the flesh, and others not at all. But these facts do not entail the relativistic thesis that no inference is really more rational than any other, or that all standards of evidence are equally good. For this thesis is itself, a value judgement; the relativist must have his own criteria for judging the rationality of inferences and standards of evidence, and his criteria are so peculiar that they assign equal merit to all standards and inferences indiscriminantly. Otherwise he could not have determined by any process of evaluation that all standards of evidence are equally good. But this is surely a good reason to reject his strange criteria, especially since he can offer us no reason to prefer his criteria to any others. To think that all types of consideration count as equally strong evidence is to have a disposition to be equally convinced by all types of consideration; but none of the facts which the relativist adduces can actually entail the prescription to accord equal weight to all types of evidence. And even according to his own theory, these facts do not support relativism more strongly than they support a rival theory that grades some standards of evidence more highly than others.

Finally, some have tried to show, by an appeal merely to the meanings of words, that certain facts necessarily provide evidence for certain conclusions:

> If it is now asked: But how *can* previous experience be a ground for assuming that such-and-such will occur later on? – the answer is: What general concept have we of grounds for this kind of assumption? This sort of statement about the past is simply what we call a ground for assuming that this will happen in the future (L. Wittgenstein, *Philosophical Investigations*, Pt. I, sec. 480.)[8]

Imagine that some were to say: 'By the very definition of the word "reason", the fact that the Koran says that Mohammed is God's prophet provides strong reason to believe that he is God's prophet.' If I have no tendency to be convinced that Mohammed is God's prophet merely by the fact that the Koran says so, then defining that fact to be a 'reason' will only force me to say: 'Granted that the testimony of the Koran is, in your sense of the word, a "reason" to believe what it says, yet I cannot see *why* anyone should believe something just because there is strong *reason* to believe it.' But the question 'Granted there is strong reason to believe it, nevertheless why should anyone believe it?' ought to be a self-answering question like 'Granted this person is a female parent, nevertheless what makes her a mother?.' Owing, however, to the naturalistic definition of 'reason' in terms of what is said in the Koran, it turns out to be an open question instead. For if the testimony of the Koran does not convince me, then defining that testimony to be a 'reason' will not convince me either; I will simply be forced to have the same doubts about the relevance of 'reasons' that I initially had about the relevance of the Koran.

Wittgenstein writes:

> If anyone said that information about the past could not convince him that something would happen in the future, I should not understand him. One might ask him: what do you expect to be told, then? What sort of information do you call a ground for such a belief? What do you call "conviction"? In what kind of way do you expect to be convinced? – If *these* are not grounds, then what are grounds? – If you say these are not grounds, then you must surely be able to state what must be the case for us to have right to say that there are grounds for our assumption. (Ibid., sec. 481)

Now, there is no problem in understanding what such a person *means* when he says he is not convinced by inductive arguments based on information about the past; what we don't understand is why he is not convinced, but that is a question for neurologists and not for philosophers. Such a person need have no difficulty in saying what he does count as grounds for beliefs about the future. He might tell us that his beliefs are based on the prophesies of the Koran, or the Bible, or the horoscope. And if we persuade him that he has all along been misusing the terms 'reason' and 'ground', then we will succeed only in altering the way he talks, not the way he thinks.

On the other hand, if we are to ensure that a person necessarily has a tendency to be convinced by what he deems to be good evidence then we must not *define* good evidence in terms of the sorts of considerations that actually do tend to convince us (owing to our contingent psychological constitution). When we say that certain considerations are good evidence for a conclusion we must not be *stating any fact* about those considerations. And this requirement will be accommodated if we are instead *prescribing* that we have a certain degree of conviction because of those considerations.

4   Ethical Naturalism *De Re*

Ethical Naturalism is currently being resurrected on the basis of recent work in the theory of truth-conditions for statements of identity and necessity.[1] By 'Ethical Naturalism' I mean any theory which holds that to call actions right or wrong, and their consequences good or bad, is to ascribe to them certain properties or relations, and that what we say about actions and their consequences when we call them right or wrong, good or bad, is true if they have these characteristics and false if they don't. By defining Naturalism in this hopefully not too arbitrary manner I intend chiefly to contrast it with a theory which might be called 'imperativism' according to which a sentence like 'It is always wrong to do X' means 'Don't anyone ever do X', from which it follows that to call an action wrong is not to say anything true or false about it, or to ascribe any characteristics to it, but is simply to forbid it universally.

Previous arguments against Naturalism had concentrated on establishing a distinction between evaluative and non-evaluative discourse, and on showing that sentences containing explicitly evaluative expressions such as 'good', 'bad', 'right' and 'wrong' could not be synonymous with sentences employing only terminology that was evaluatively neutral. But the form of Naturalism which threatens a revival does not deny this. It holds in common with its adversaries that there is a distinction between description and evaluation, and that no evaluative utterance is synonymous with a non-evaluative one; but it maintains that the properties and relations ascribed to things by evaluative utterances may nevertheless be the same as those ascribed by non-evaluative utterances. That the sentences ascribing those properties are not synonymous is one thing; that the properties ascribed are not identical is another matter. And it supports this claim by pointing to the impressive case which can be made for holding that even in non-evaluative discourse the properties ascribed to a thing are not always distinct where the ascriptions are not synonymous; and for all that has been shown by any anti-Naturalistic argument so far advanced, evaluative discourse might be similar in precisely this respect. To see how little is to be gained by this tactic and how much more implausible than even the old form of Naturalism it turns out to be, we will first review the familiar arguments against the 'Naturalistic Fallacy' and then see exactly where the new theory leads.

NATURALISM AND REAL DEFINITIONS

Early in the exposition of his 'Open Question Argument', G. E. Moore asks: 'What, then, is good? How is good to be defined?' (*Principia Ethica*, p. 6). He answers that it cannot be defined at all and that is the end of the matter. But he hastens to add that he does not intend this question to be a request for a purely verbal definition of the word 'good', since we can and often do say what 'good' means: the English word 'good' means the same as the French word 'bon'. If a Frenchman asks "Que veut dire le mot anglais 'good'?" and receives the answer "Ça veut dire 'bon'", he has been told what the word 'good' means.

> A definition does indeed often mean the expression of one word's meaning in other words. But this is not the sort of definition I am asking for. Such a definition can never be of ultimate importance in any study except lexicography. (Ibid., p.6)

It is merely an accident of linguistic history, without any philosophical importance whatever, that English has no latinate synonym for the Saxon word 'good' in the way that 'fair', which is of Saxon origin, has the Latin synonym 'just'. If English had developed differently and incorporated, like French, a form of the word 'bonum', then it would have been as easy to say what 'good' means as it is to say that 'justice' means the same as 'fairness'. But the ability to define 'good' in this sort of way is of no value to philosophy since even a person with no prior knowledge of English could decode enough of the language to know that 'justice' and 'fairness' mean the same thing and yet have no idea what it is that they both mean. And even if we did know what 'good' means, in a way that is unavailable to the decoder who knows only that it means the same as some other word he does not understand, we would still not have the knowledge that interests Moore. He is not at the moment concerned with the meaning of the word 'good':

> My business is not with its proper usage as established by custom. I should, indeed, be foolish, if I tried to use it for something which it did not usually denote . . . I shall, therefore, use the word in the sense in which I think it is ordinarily used; but at the same time I am not anxious to discuss whether I am right in thinking that it is so used. My business is solely with that object or idea, which I hold, rightly or wrongly, that the word is generally used to stand for. What I want to discover is the nature of that object or idea. (Ibid., p.6)

According to the traditional distinction between real and verbal definitions, a verbal definition tells what a word means, while real definition ('real' from the Latin *res* = 'thing') tells what the thing is which the word happens to stand for. And this is apparently just the distinction Moore has in mind:
Definitions of the kind which I am asking for [are]

> definitions which describe the real nature of the object or notion denoted by a word, and which do not merely tell us what the word is used to mean. (Ibid., p. 7)

The difference between knowing what a word means and knowing the 'real nature' of the thing which the word denotes is not difficult to illustrate: we all know that the word 'gravity' denotes whatever is responsible for the tendency of terrestial objects to fall towards the centre of the earth; but no one knows exactly what is responsible for this tendency. So, although we know the meaning of the word 'gravity', we do not know the real nature of the thing which the word denotes. In the same way, if the expression 'intrinsic goodness' meant 'whatever ought to be aimed at for its own sake' we could certainly know that it meant this without having any idea what it was that we ought to aim at for its own sake. A verbal definition of something specifies what Locke calls its 'nominal essence' which is a set of features, often including a role or function, that uniquely characterizes the thing and can be used (if anything can) to identify it. A real definition states what it is that turns out to be uniquely identified by the description given in the nominal definition. The two definitions are not generally synonymous, and the 'real essence' consists of properties which are usually distinct from those contained in the nominal essence.

Now although Moore subscribes, in the plainest possible terms, to the distinction between real and verbal definitions, and has indicated that his concern is with the former, yet there is something unclear in what he says. When he professes to be interested in the object or idea denoted by 'good' one may wonder whether he is using the word 'idea' in the Platonic sense in which it means, not a thought in the mind, but an independently existing abstract object. But in the next breath he speaks of the 'object or notion' and we are left in no doubt· that by 'idea' he means a mental entity. The question then arises whether he is after the object itself or our notion of it. My idea or notion of Catiline may be different from Cicero's, and yet the person of whom there are these different notions is the same in each case. Similarly, even if we all had the same notion of goodness it would seem that the question could still arise whether it was a misleading notion; and that could only be settled by comparing goodness itself with our notion of it. But as soon as we try to do this we are confronted with Meno's Paradox. For in order to 'find' the property we are 'looking for' so that we can compare it with our notion, we must be able to recognize it when we come across it; and if our only means of identifying it is a notion that is inaccurate to begin with then we will be misled to some other property instead of goodness. The only way I can see to avoid being caught in the paradox is simply to stipulate that the property being sought is whatever property happens to fit our notion or a substantial part of it. This will certainly ensure that we never have a false notion of goodness, but it will necessarily restrict that notion to the nominal essence of goodness: such a stipulation will only provide a means of identifying the property we are talking about; but, like the verbal definition of 'gravity', it will not tell us the 'real nature' of that property.

THE OPEN QUESTION ARGUMENT

Moore's refutation of Naturalism and his exposure of the 'naturalistic fallacy' are supposed to be accomplished by means of the Open Question Argument. But it is crucial to the power of this argument whether it proves that goodness itself is distinct from, say, pleasure, or merely that our notion of goodness is distinct from our notion of pleasure.

First of all, what precisely is the naturalistic fallacy supposed to be? Upon inspection it turns out be the sort of confusion that Plato was trying to clear up in the early dialogues about Socratic definitions.

Euthyphro is asked what piety is and answers that it is just what he is doing now, prosecuting his father for criminal negligence in the death of a hired labourer. Socrates points out that many other actions are pious as well, and that what he is asking for is the single feature by virtue of which all pious actions are pious, so that knowing this he would be able to tell of any action which class it fell into. After a while Euthyphro decides that piety is what all the gods love, and impiety is what they all hate. This is at least closer to the sort of answer required, but Socrates argues that even though all and only pious actions are also actions which the gods love, nevertheless piety and being loved by the gods are two different properties which are constantly conjoined, and not one and the same property. The property about which Socrates is inquiring is not merely one which is common and peculiar to all pious actions but the feature by virtue of which they are all pious. It must be the quality whose possession makes something pious. This quality, whatever it turns out to be, is what Socrates calls 'piety itself'.

The same can be said about a question like 'What is (intrinsically) good?.' It might quite naturally, and sometimes correctly be taken to be a request for an inventory of good things, so that one might answer: 'Pleasure is good, so is knowledge, health, ... ' But this is not an answer to the question Moore has in mind. Nor would it do just to point out a characteristic which distinguished good things from everything else, i.e. a characteristic which all and only good things had. The question is intended to be a request for the definition of goodness, just as with Socrates it was a request for the definition of piety. And the definition of a quality must not be confused with an enumeration of other qualities which happen to be common and peculiar to everything which has the first one.

> Yet a mistake of this simple kind has commonly been made about 'good'. It may be true that all things which are good are *also* something else, just as it is true that all things which are yellow produce a certain kind of vibration in the light. And it is a fact, that Ethics aims at discovering what are those other properties belonging to all things which are good. But far too many philosophers have thought that when they named those other properties they were actually defining good; that these properties, in fact, were simply not 'other', but absolutely and entirely the same with goodness. This view I propose to call the 'naturalistic fallacy'. (Ibid., p. 10)

So the fallacy is that of inferring from the premise that certain features are always present where goodness is, and are not present elsewhere, that these features are the same thing as goodness. And this sort of fallacy is not peculiar to ethics. All and only things which are X may also be Y, but it does not follow that for something to be X is the same as for it to be Y. For although there *is* no X which is not also Y, we have not been told whether there could be something which was one but not the other.

But why can we not find some properties, call them Xness, Yness, and Zness, which are not only common and peculiar to all good things, but are also the properties which *make* things good, that is, are identical with the property goodness? Then we could construct a real definition of intrinsic goodness which would have the form 'To be intrinsically good is the same as to be X, Y, and Z.' Moore believes that this is impossible, and that the only real definition of goodness is the empty tautology 'Good is good.' This is because he takes goodness to be one of the simple, unanalysable properties in terms of which other properties are defined but which itself cannot be defined without circularity in terms of others. His arguments for this view, however, appear to rest on the grossest confusion of real and verbal definitions, a distinction which he was at such pains to establish previously.

What are his arguments? Suppose someone ventures a definition of intrinsic goodness such as, for instance, 'To be good is to be a harmless pleasure.' Moore will then say:

> whatever definition be offered, it may always be asked, with significance, of the complex so defined, whether it is itself good. (Ibid., p. 15)

Thus we can ask 'Is a harmless pleasure, after all, a good thing?' and this will be a significant question, unlike 'Is a good thing a good thing?' or 'Is a harmless pleasure a harmless pleasure?.' Now although some fanatical puritans may consider pleasure to be evil because it distracts our attention from God, yet for all I know it may still turn out that all and only things which are intrinsically good have the property of being a harmelss pleasure;

> but it is very doubtful whether this is the case, and the mere fact that we understand what is meant by doubting it, shews clearly that we have two different notions before our minds. (Ibid., p. 16)

The notions may be different, clearly. Sergeant Garcia's notion of the daring and elusive Zorro was certainly different from his notion of the lazy and effeminate Don Diego dela Vega. But this did not make El Zorro himself someone other than Don Diego. What Moore must show is not that the notions are different – that can be admitted easily enough. He must show that the things of which we have such notions are themselves different. Our notion of goodness may indeed be different from our notion of being a harmless pleasure. But is goodness itself something other than the characteristic of being a harmless pleasure? That is what we wish to know.

'But,' Moore continues,

> whoever will attentively consider with himself what is actually before his mind when he asks the question 'Is pleasure (or whatever it may be) after all good?' can easily satisfy himself that he is not merely wondering whether pleasure is pleasure. . . . Everyone does in fact understand the question 'Is this good?'. When he thinks of it, his state of mind is different from what it would be, were he asked 'Is this pleasant, or desired, or approved?'. It has a distinct meaning for him. (Ibid., pp. 16–17.)

This is reasonably clear, but what does it show? Anyone who attentively considers what is actually before his mind when he asks 'Is Hesperus after all indentical with Phosphorus?' may be sure that he is not merely wondering whether Hesperus is Hesperus. The two questions have distinct meanings. Yet this could not be used to show that Hesperus is distinct from Phosphorus. How is the argument any better in ethics?

> Whenever /anyone/ thinks of 'intrinsic value' or 'intrinsic worth', or says a thing 'ought to exist', he has before his mind the unique object – the unique property of things – which I mean by 'good'. Everybody is constantly aware of this notion, although he may never become aware at all that it is different from other notions of which he is also aware. (Ibid., p. 17)

This is the fruit of the confusion that was sown earlier. We have before our minds a certain object, namely goodness, which is a property of things. Moore then says we are constantly 'aware of this notion'. What notion?! Certainly not goodness; it is a property. Are properties then to be considered notions in the head? Notions are ideas in the mind and did not exist before there were minds to put them into. And yet things had properties and characteristics before there were minds; grass had the property of being green and water had the property of being wet before anyone had a notion of these things or features. We require an explanation of how this could be so if properties are ideas in the mind. I should point out that I am not relying on a Platonistic view of properties as abstract entities. Although I have contrasted our notions of things with the independently existing objects of which they are notions, e.g. Catiline, Zorro, Hesperus and Phosphorus, the only sense in which I require there to be such a thing as greenness independently of our thoughts is the anti-Platonistic sense in which there are green *things* independently of our thoughts.

Moore's argument so far seems to be that if the word 'good' meant the same as the word 'pleasant', then the words 'Is what is pleasant good?' would mean the same as the words 'Is what is pleasant pleasant?'. But the first set of words is used to ask a significant and sensible question while the second is not, and so the two sets of words cannot mean the same thing. The first question is an open one; that is, when, we have found out that a thing is pleasant it is still an open question whether it is good. The second question is not an open one; once we have found out that a thing is pleasant, it is a self-answering question to ask whether it is pleasant. This same argument may be found in the first chapter of Richard Price's *Review of the Principle Questions of Morals* (3rd ed., 1787; ed. D. D. Raphael, OUP, 1974).

Right and wrong when applied to actions which are commanded or forbidden by the will of God, or that produce good or harm, do not signify merely, that such actions are commanded or forbidden, or that they are useful or hurtful, but a *sentiment* concerning them and our consequent approbation or disapprobation of the performance of them. Were this not true, it would be palpably absurd in any case to ask, whether it is *right* to obey a command, or *wrong* to disobey it; and the propositions, *obeying a command is right*, or *producing happiness is right*, would be most trifling, as expressing no more than that obeying a command, is obeying a command, or producing happiness is producing happiness.(pp. 16–17)

What conclusion does Moore wish to draw from this argument?

There is no meaning in saying that pleasure is good, unless good is

something different from pleasure. . . . It will always remain pertinent to ask whether the feeling itself is good; and if so, then good
cannot itself be identical with any feeling. (*op. cit.*, pp. 14, 41)

This passage, however, is not easy to understand, principally because
it is ungrammatical: the last occurance of the word 'good' appears to
be the subject of the sentence 'Good cannot be identical with any
feeling'; but only nouns or noun phrases can be the subject of a
sentence, while 'good' is an adjective. So I shall take this to mean
that the property good*ness* is not identical with any feeling. But now
it is difficult to understand the previous remark, that there is no
meaning in saying that pleasure is good unless good (?) is something
different from pleasure. To begin with, the issue is not whether
pleasure is good, but whether pleasure (or rather pleasant*ness*) is
identical with good*ness*, or whether pleasant things are thereby good
things. And to argue that pleasantness (i.e. the *property* of being
pleasant) is distinct from goodness on the ground that we can doubt
that pleasantness is good, is as absurd as to argue that 3-sidedness is
distinct from triangularity because we can doubt whether 3-sidedness
is triangular. Certainly 3-sided things are triangular, but 3-sidedness
itself is a property and therefore has no shape at all, so of course it is
not triangular. And if we can avoid the Platonistic self-predication
involved in wondering whether triangularity is triangular then we can
also refrain from asking whether pleasantness is itself pleasant,
whether goodness is good, and even whether pleasantness is good.

I think we must in the end take Moore to be arguing that since it
always remains pertinent to ask whether pleasant things are good it
follows that goodness cannot be identical with pleasantness. The
validity of this inference is anything but obvious. Gilbert Harman, in
The Nature of Morality (OUP, 1977), objects that if the Open
Question Argument were valid it could be used to do *a priori*
chemistry:

> An analogous argument could be used on someone who was
> ignorant of the chemical structure of water to "prove" to him that
> water is not H_2O. This person will agree that it is not an open
> question whether water is water but it is an open question, at least
> for him, whether water is H_2O. Since this argument would not show
> that water is not H_2O, the open question argument in ethics cannot
> be used as it stands to show that for an act to be an act that ought to
> be done is not for it to have some natural characteristic C. (p. 19)

Our notion of a thing's being water was certainly different from our notion of its having the chemical structure H_2O, and yet we would not have inferred that water itself does not have the structure H_2O. But one must be careful here. Moore would certainly agree that all and only stuff that was water was stuff with the structure H_2O. Yet he would insist that everything that was water was *also* H_2O, that to be water and to be H_2O were two different properties which happened to be constantly conjoined, like being yellow and reflecting light of a certain wave-length. And he would insist that it was the Open Question Argument itself which showed that, although they were co-extensive properties, they must be distinct.

Now the issue which Harman's example raises seems to me to be the one whose resolution ultimately determines whether Ethical Naturalism is possible, and therefore I propose to broach it in some detail in the following sections. The outcome of the investigation, as I attempt to show, is that Harman's example succeeds in refuting Moore's Open Question Argument *only if* there exist such abstract objects as chemical structures in addition to the various chemically structured material substances.

NECESSARY IDENTITY – NAMES AND DESCRIPTIONS

Moore would argue that because one could know that water was water without knowing whether water was H_2O it follows that to be water is not the same as to be H_2O. But here is an example where a similar argument would not be valid. Ahasuerus was the ancient king of Persia who, according to the Old Testament book of *Esther*, divorced his faithless queen and commanded the most beautiful women throughout the empire to be sought out and assembled at his court so that he could choose a new wife; the jewish girl Esther appealed to him so much that she became his queen and eventually saved her people from destruction when the King's anger was aroused against them by the deception of his unscrupulous prime minister. Xerxes I was the Persian king whose army was delayed by the Spartans at Thermopylae and who was finally defeated at Salamis by the Athenian fleet commanded by Themistocles. Most scholars believe that Xerxes and Ahasuerus were the same person, although some think that Ahasuerus was Artaxerxes II. But from the fact that when we wonder whether Ahasuerus was Xerxes we are not just wondering whether Ahasuerus was Ahasuerus, it obviously does not follow that Ahasuerus was not identical with Xerxes.

A defender of the Open Question Argument would no doubt concede that it cannot be used to prove *a priori* that Ahasuerus and Xerxes were different people, but would probably claim that there is something else which it does prove. The Persian King who married Esther may have been identical with the Persian king who was defeated at Salamis; but it would be alleged that the argument shows (1) that *to be* the Persian king who married Esther is not the same as *to be* the Persian king who lost at Salamis, and consequently (2) that the king who married Esther and the king who lost at Salamis might have been different people even if in fact they were identical. This corresponds to the earlier claim that although all and only water is (for the sake of argument) H_2O, nevertheless to be water is not the same as to be H_2O and therefore water might have turned out to be something else, even though it didn't.

Now sentences (1) and (2) are open to different interpretations; on one interpretation they express true propositions, but on another they express false propositions. Sentence (1) says something true if it means:

(1*)   *To occupy* the throne of Persia and *to have married* Esther is not the same as *to occupy* the throne of Persia and *to have been defeated* at Salamis.

This sentence contains expressions which refer to thrones, empires, women, and battles; but it contains no expression referring to any king. Sentence (1) contains the definite descriptions 'the king of Persia who married Esther' and 'the king of Persia who lost at Salamis', and these might naturally be thought to refer to a king of Persia. If they do then (1) is false. For to be identical with, or the same person as, the king of Persia who married Esther is just to be a certain man, viz. whoever is referred to by the description 'the king of Persia who married Esther', namely Ahasuerus. And to be the same man as the king of Persia who was defeated at Salamis is simply to be Xerxes. It is *not* to have occupied any throne, or married any woman, or lost any battle. For surely if anyone was identical with the person who did these things, it was Xerxes, and he was certainly identical with this person when he was two years old and had not yet claimed the throne, married Esther, or fought battles. In fact, he might have been that person and never have done any of these things;

he might easily have been murdered in infancy as Cyrus the Great nearly was.

There is a certain person with whom we identify Xerxes, and to specify who this person is we mention certain things that he did; we say: he is the person who did those things. But Xerxes was that person before he did those things and would have been that person even if he had never lived to do them. Therefore doing those things is no part of being that person. There is a person, such that to be the king of Persia who married Esther is simply to be that person; and there is a person, such that to be the king of Persia who was defeated at Salamis is again simply to be that person; and it is to be the same person in each case. Therefore, contrary to what (1) says if the descriptions are used referentially, to be the Persian king who married Esther really *is* the same as to be the Persian king who lost at Salamis.

Sentence (2) says something true if it means:

> (2*) The Persian king who married Esther might not have been defeated at Salamis; some other Persian king might have been defeated there instead.

In this sentence there is only one expression which can plausibly be said to refer to a king, namely, 'the Persian king who married Esther'. The phrase 'some other Persian king' does not refer to some other Persian king. For if it did, which one would it be? There is nothing to make it refer to one king rather than another, and therefore there is nothing to make it refer to any king at all.[2] So this sentence does not say of any king that he might not have been identical with the king who married Esther. But sentence (2) does, if both definite descriptions are taken to refer to what satisfies them, in which case what sentence (2) says is false. For consider the sentence:

> (3) The king of Persia who married Esther was not identical with the king of Persia who was defeated at Salamis.

Everyone agrees that if this sentence expresses a true proposition then so does the sentence which results from it when the definite descriptions are replaced by names which refer to the referents of those descriptions. If the majority of scholars are correct then both descriptions refer to Xerxes. Thus if (3) expresses a true proposition, so does

(4) Xerxes was not identical with Xerxes.

But what (4) says is false; it not only *is not* true, it *could not* be true. Neither, therefore, could what (3) says be true.

Again, consider this sentence, which is essentially the same as (2):

(5) The king of Persia who married Esther might not have been identical with the king of Persia who lost at Salamis.

I would also say of this sentence that if it says something true then so does the sentence which results from it by replacing the definite descriptions with names which refer to the same things. So if (5) expresses a true proposition, so does

(6) Xerxes might not have been identical with Xerxes.

What (6) says is obviously false; therefore what (5) says is false as well. This last argument will probably not convince those who think that modal expressions such as 'possibly' and 'necessarily', 'might' and 'must' introduce non-extensional contexts, i.e. contexts where the substitution of co-referential terms does not preserve truth. I agree that, from the fact that the name 'Sir Walter Scott' and the description 'the author of *Waverley*' refer to the same man, and the fact that the sentence 'George IV wondered whether Scott was the author of *Waverley*' expresses a true proposition, it does not follow that we can substitute the description for the name and conclude that 'George IV wondered whether the author of *Waverley* was the author of *Waverley*' also expresses a true proposition. Russell has made that much clear. But I am not aware of any good reason to suppose that modal expressions are in this respect like verbs for propositional attitudes.

Consider the sentence:

(6) The king of Persia who married Esther was necessarily identical with the king of Persia who lost at Salamis.

I think most of the people who believe that (6) is false do so because they mistakenly think it implies:

(7) The Persian king who married Esther necessarily lost at Salamis.

But (6) says the king was necessarily a certain person, while (7) says that he necessarily did certain things. *Who a person was* and *what he did* are logically independent of each other, even if we can only say who he was by saying what he did. Suppose someone thinks that he can say something true by uttering the sentence:

(8) If some Persian king other than Ahasuerus had lost the Battle of Salamis then the Persian king who married Esther would not have been identical with the Persian king who lost the Battle of Salamis.

We need only ask such a person which king he thinks he is referring to, if any, by the description 'the Persian king who lost the Battle of Salamis'. If he is referring to a king at all, should he not use it like the rest of us to refer to what *fits* the description? What excuse is there for trying to use it to refer to something which might have or would have, but in fact does not fit it? If he is not referring to Xerxes, then what could there be about his use of the description by virtue of which he would be referring to someone in particular among all the people in the world there are to refer to?

It might be objected that any proposition of the form 'x would have been the F' entails a corresponding proposition of the form 'x would have been uniquely F' and hence 'x would have been F', just as 'x is the F' entails 'x is uniquely F' and 'x is F'. And consequently, to say

(9) Ahasuerus would still have been (identical with) the king who lost at Salamis even if he had not lost at Salamis,

is to imply the contradictory proposition

(10) Ahasuerus would still have lost at Salamis even if he had not lost at Salamis.

From this we are meant to draw the conclusion (a) that if 'x is F' had been false then 'x is the F' would also have been false, and (b) that since 'x would have been F' is false, so is 'x would have been the F'.

But (a) is false. All that is true is that if 'x is F' *is* false then so is 'x is the F'; of this we are assured by Modus Tollens. But Modus Tollens does not licence the counter-factual inference: if 'x is F' *had been* false, then 'x is the F' *would have been* false. On the contrary, if 'x is F' had been false then 'x is the F' would not even have existed. It is true that if the proposition expressed by the sentence

(11)   Ahasuerus lost the Battle of Salamis

had been false, then the sentence

(12)   Ahasuerus was the king who lost the Battle of Salamis

would also have expressed *a* false proposition, but *not* the one it expresses now. For, given the actual course of the world's history, if the desription 'the king who lost the Battle of Salamis' refers to anyone at all it refers to Ahasuerus, while if the proposition expressed by (11) had been false and some other king had lost, then the description would have referred to somebody else and not to Ahasuerus. In that case (12) *would have* expressed a proposition about two people, whereas the proposition it *does* express is about a single person, Ahasuerus. So the proposition that *would have been* expressed and the proposition that *actually is* expressed are two different propositions since they are not even about the same people. The sense of sentence (12) would be the same in both situations, but since the reference is different the propositions expressed are different. For instance, the sentence 'I am older than you' has the same sense no matter who utters it, for it is true just in case the speaker is older than the audience addressed (no matter who these happen to be). But since the reference varies from person to person, so, obviously, does the proposition expressed.

If Artaxerxes I had lost the Battle of Salamis then sentence (12) would have referred both to him and to Ahasuerus. There would have been no sentence which had both the sense and the reference of the sentence as it is used now. No one would have been able to express the proposition we now use that sentence to express, using the description referentially; if you like, the proposition would not have existed. Perhaps a better way of putting it would be to use Wilfrid Sellar's device of dot-quotation and say that no sentence would have been an •Ahasuerus was identical with the Persian king who lost the Battle of Salamis•, where to be such an utterance is to be a sentence-token with the same sense and reference which (12) happens to have.[3] So if a necessary truth is a proposition (platonistically speaking) which is true in every possible world in which it exists, then (12) expresses a necessary truth if it expresses a truth at all. Or, taking propositions to be kinds of sentence-tokens (nominalistically speaking), a necessary truth is a sort of sentence-token such that nothing can be a token of that sort and be false. And in any possible world in which some sentence-token is an •Ahasuerus was identical with the Persian king who lost the Battle of Salamis', that sentence-token is true. (It is an interesting consequence of this analysis that (12), which is a necessary truth, entails (11), which is only a contingent truth. This is because, although (11) is true in every possible world in which (12) exists or is expressible, nevertheless it is false in some of the worlds in which (12) does not exist.)

That is why principle (a) is false. But what about (b)? This is the principle that since 'x would have been the F' entails 'x would have been F', if the latter is false so is the former. It seems to me that (b) is false as well, if the description 'the F' is used referentially, for in that case 'x would have been the F' does not entail 'x would have been F'. Sentence (9), for example, says *who* Ahasuerus would still have *been* even if he had not lost the battle, while (10) says *what* he would still have *done* even if he had not done it. Ahasuerus would still have been the person who, as it happens, *did* lose the battle even if things had been different and he *had not* lost it; for there is obviously no other person distinct from Ahasuerus with whom he would have been identical instead. At this point I can only say that since (9) is true and (10) is false, (9) does not entail (10).

So far I have been dealing mainly with identity statements involving definite descriptions. But I think exactly the same moves can be made with respect to proper names as well since I think, with Russell, that they are synonymous with the description or cluster of descriptions used to identify their bearers.[4] The only argument I have seen to the contrary is one used in various places by David Wiggins.[5]

> Take the name 'Aristotle'. If Aristotle might not have been the pupil of Plato or the teacher of Alexander then no such description has a sense suitable to constitute (however useful it may be to help *specify*) the sense of Aristotle's name. But it is descriptions like these which Frege seems to wish to supply to perform the sense conferring role.
>
> The general form of the difficulty is this. Let ø be any candidate whatever to be a specification or citation of the sense of a proper name n_1, and sufficient to determine its reference. Then, where b_1 is n_1's bearer, "if there is any such thing as b_1, b_1 is ø" could not, if ø gave or analysed the very *sense* of n_1, be false. But a statement such as this, predicating ø of b_1 (if b_1 is an ordinary particular and not, say, a number, and if ø picks out just b_1), cannot be any better than contingent. So genuine proper names cannot have their sense in the manner which Frege's theory apparently requires them to have it. ('Frege's Problem of the Morning Star . . .', p. 222)

Suppose, for the sake of argument, that the proper name 'Aristotle', in one of its uses, is synonymous with the simple description 'the teacher of Alexander', and consider the two sentences:

(13)   Aristotle taught Alexander,
(14)   The teacher of Alexander taught Alexander.

Wiggins' argument is that (14) expresses a proposition which could not be false; and if (14) is synonymous with (13), then so does (13); but the proposition expressed by (13) might have been false since Aristotle might never have taught Alexander; therefore (13) is not synonymous with (14). To explain what is wrong with this argument I think it is necessary to appeal to some distinction between *de re* and *de dicto* modality. Compare:

(15)   The teacher of Alexander might not have taught Alexander,
(16)   It might have been false that the teacher of Alexander taught Alexander.

Although, as I have argued, the teacher of Alexander could not have *been* anyone else than the person who did teach Alexander, nevertheless he might have *done* something other than teach Alexander; he might have taught someone else instead, or never have taught at all. So the proposition expressed by (15) is true. But it does not follow that if the teacher of Alexander had not taught Alexander then the proposition expressed by (14) would have been false; on the contrary, that proposition would not even have existed (or, at least, would not have been expressible). If someone other than Aristotle had taught Alexander then the description in sentence (14) would have referred to him instead, and (14) would have been used to say something true about that person, but not about Aristotle. And since the proposition that *would have been* expressed would not even have been about Aristotle, it can't be identical with the proposition that *is* expressed, which is about Aristotle. If two sentences do not even refer to the same things, they cannot express the same proposition. On the other hand, some other description would have served just as well to pick out Aristotle, but any sentence containing it would not have had the same sense as (14); and if two sentences don't have the same sense, they cannot express the same proposition. That is why the proposition expressed by (16) is false.

Similarly, if Aristotle, had never taught Alexander, he might still have had the name 'Aristotle'; but his name would have had a different sense. Sentence (13) would still have been used to assert a proposition about Aristotle (a false one), but not the proposition it is now used to express. If someone else named 'Aristotle' had taught Alexander then that person's name might have had the same sense as Aristotle's name now possesses (on our simplistic assumption), and in that case sentence (13) would have had the sense it now has. But it would not have had the same reference. Either way, sentence (13) would not have expressed the same proposition it does now, for that proposition would have been inexpressible. That is why, although Aristotle might not have taught Alexander, the proposition that Aristotle taught Alexander could not have been false.

THE RIGID DESIGNATION OF ABSTRACT OBJECTS

I have been arguing that the Open Question Argument cannot validly be applied to refute identity statements expressed in sentences which employ proper names and definite descriptions used referentially. This raises a question about expressions which are not obviously used to refer to anything, but which nevertheless seem to share certain properties with referring expressions. I wish to say of such phrases as 'one metre long' that, *pace* Kripke,[6] when they are used to describe a counter-factual state of affairs they "designate" the properties we currently use them to ascribe, and not the properties they would have been used to ascribe if the counter-factual situation had been actual. But unless these expressions really do refer to properties and relations, just as proper names and definite descriptions refer to ordinary material objects, then we cannot explain why they designate the *same* properties in describing hypothetical circumstances in the way we explain the constant designation of names and descriptions.

To see how the problem arises, consider a remark by Sir Arthur Eddington on why the Standard Metre in Paris is necessarily one metre long and could not have been any other length.

Do not bring in the idea of change of length in describing the apparatus for defining length. Obviously the adopted standard of length cannot change length, whatever it is made of. If a meter is defined as the length of a certain bar, that bar can never be anything but a metre long; and if we assert that this bar changes length, it is clear that we must have changed our minds as to the definition of length. (*Space, Time, and Gravitation*, CUP, 1920, p. 4)

Let us suppose that we have defined the *meaning* of the expression 'one metre long' in terms of the Standard Metre in Paris at some particular time t_0, so that the sentence-form

(17) x is one metre long

means simply

(18) x is as long as S was at t_0,

where 'S' is the name of the Standard Metre stick. Someone might be tempted to conclude that, from the very meaning of the terms, S could never have been anything but one metre long at t_0; for no matter how long it had been, it would always have been just as long as itself. Yet it is difficult to believe that being chosen the standard of length could make S impervious to the effects of heat and cold. If other metal bars contract when chilled, why would not the Standard Metre have contracted if it had been chilled to the same temperature?

What seems perfectly obvious is that if S had been chilled to a low temperature it would have been shorter than it was, and hence shorter than one metre. Yet the sentence

(19) S was one metre long at t_0

would still have expressed a necessary truth. The question is whether it would have expressed the same proposition we now use it to express, or some other proposition instead. Let me briefly explore an avenue trodden by Professor Kripke to see whether it leads to a satisfactory answer.

According to Kripke, what leads people to think that the standard of length cannot itself change length is taking the definition of 'one metre long' to give the meaning of that expression instead of to fix its *reference*. If someone stipulates that one metre is to be the length of S at a fixed time t_0, then he is

using this definition not to *give the meaning* of what he called the 'metre', but to *fix the reference*. (For such an abstract thing as a unit of length, the notion of reference may be unclear. But let's suppose it's clear enough for present purposes.) He uses it to fix a reference. There is a certain length which he wants to mark out. He marks it out by an accidental property, namely that there is a stick of that length. . . . There is no conflict between the counterfactual statement /that if S had been heated at t_0 it would have been longer than one metre/ and the definition of 'one metre' as 'the length of S at t_0', because the 'definition', properly understood, does not say that the phrase 'one metre' is to be synonymous . . . with the phrase 'the length of S at t_0', but rather that we have *determined the reference* of the phrase 'one metre' by stipulating that 'one metre' is to be a rigid designator of the length which is in fact the length of S at t_0. ('Naming and Necessity' in G. Harman and D. Davidson (eds), *Semantics of Natural Language*, Reidel, 1972, pp. 274–5.)

If we follow Kripke, we may say that there exists a certain length which S had at t_0, and we can use the phrase 'the length of S at t_0' to refer to it. But there is no need to deny that this phrase used referentially is synonymous with the expression 'one metre'. For when we use the description as a referring expression we use it to refer to the length which S actually had at t_0, not the length (which one?!) it might have had or would have had if things had been different. S might not have had the length it did have at t_0, in which case some other length would have been named 'one metre'. The sentence 'One metre is the length of S at t_0' would still have expressed a true proposition, but not the proposition we now use it to express. For the sentence would have been used to refer to a different length; and if the proposition we would have expressed is not even about the same length as the one we do express, they cannot be the same proposition. So if S had been hotter or colder at t_0 than it was, it would have been longer or shorter than one metre, even though the *sentence* 'S had a length of one metre at t_0' would have expressed (some other) necessary truth.

This explanation requires that we can refer to such abstract entities as lengths, and what this amounts to is not very clear at all, as Kripke acknowledges. Nor is it clear what the relation is between the abstract length of one metre and all the concrete metre sticks which 'have' that length, as Plato showed (*Parmenides*, 130e–131e). Yet without the abstract objects the explanation fails. For suppose that instead of saying things of the form 'x has the length which S had at t_0 we utter sentences such as (18): 'x is just as long as S was at t_0'. If we speak in this way we shall not even appear to be making reference to anything other than S, the moment t_0 (assuming that there are such things), and the object x being compared with S. The proposition that S was at t_0 as long as S was at t_0 is of course tautologically true. Could S have been shorter than it was? Well, no matter how long S had been, the sentence

(20)   S was at t_0 as long as S was at t_0

would still have expressed an analytic truth, but now there is no reason to doubt that it would have expressed the *same* truth that it now expresses. For the terms 'S' and 't_0' would have been used to refer to the same metal bar and the same instant which we now use them to designate; and the phrase 'as long as' would have had the same sense. Since that sentence would have had the same sense and reference which it now has, it would have expressed the same proposition it now expresses. And if (20) is synonymous with (19) 'S was one metre long at t_0', then the same proposition we now use (19) to express would have been true, and S would have been one metre long no matter how long it had been. I cannot see what sense it makes to say that S would *not* have been one metre long even though it would have been true that S *was* one metre long, and if we renounce abstract entities then I cannot see why the proposition that S was one metre long would not have been true no matter how long S had been.

Nevertheless, if S had been shorter than it was then it would not have been as long as it was, and consequently would not have been a metre long. For, to be a metre long is to be as long as S *was*, not as long as S *might* have been or *would* have been. Yet if we now assert something true by saying 'S was as long as it was, namely one metre', and would still have been asserting something true even if S had been shorter than it was, how can we show that we would have been asserting something *different* from what we actually assert by uttering that sentence? Given the supposition that (19) 'S was one metre long at t_0' is synonymous with (20) 'S was at t_0 as long as S was at t_0' there seem to be only three alternatives:

A.   S would have been one metre long no matter how long it had been,

B.   S would not have been one metre long even though it would have been true that S was one metre long,

C.   S would not have been one metre long and it would not have been true that S was one metre long.

Eddington, I think, would have been satisfied with A. B seems to me incoherent. C is what I prefer. But the only way I can see to explain even the possibility of C being true is to re-admit abstract entities in order that sentences might have different lengths to *refer* to when utterred in different counter-factual states of affairs. Then they would express different propositions which could all be true under the appropriate circumstances; for it is a complete mystery how they could be different propositions unless they were about different (abstract) things or else said something different about the same things. So, embracing this explanation I shall suggest that sentences (19) and (20) refer not only to stick S and instant t_0, but despite the appearance they also refer to a length. And I suggest that, contrary to Kripke, sentence

(21)   S had the length on metre at t_0

is synonymous with

(22)   S had at t_0 the length which S had at t_0.

What led Kripke to say that 'the length which S had at t_0' was not synonymous with the phrase 'the length one metre, but merely served to fix its reference? The reason is that he thought the expression 'one metre' was a rigid designator and the description 'the length of S at t_0' was not.

What do I mean by 'rigid designator'? I mean a term that designates the same object in all possible worlds. To get rid of one confusion which certainly is not mine, I do not use "might have designated a different object" to refer to the fact that language might have been used differently. . . . That is not what I mean. What I mean . . . *[is]* that in *our* language as *we* use it in describing a counterfactual situation, there might have been a different object satisfying the descriptive conditions *we* give for reference. So, for example, we use the phrase 'the inventor of bifocals', when we are talking about another possible world or a counterfactual situation, to refer to whoever in that counterfactual situation, would have invented bifocals . . . ('Identity and Necessity', p. 145)

Consider the sentence

(23)   If Jefferson had made Franklin's inventions, he would have
        been the inventor of bifocals.

It is obvious that (23) cannot express a true proposition if 'the
inventor of bifocals' is taken to refer to the person who *actually* fits
that description; for there are no circumstances under which Jefferson
would have been Franklin. Kripke thinks that (23) does say something true and would evidently argue that since the description
cannot refer to Franklin it must refer to Jefferson. But now compare
(23) with a similar sentence

(24)   If someone else had made Franklin's inventions, that person
        would have been the inventor of bifocals.

To whom does 'the inventor of bifocals' refer in this case? Surely not
to someone else; for the phrase 'someone else' does *not* refer to
someone else since it does not refer at all. There could not be
anything by virtue of which this phrase referred to one particular
'someone else' rather than any other 'someone else', and therefore
nothing by virtue of which it referred to anyone. Furthermore,
suppose that Franklin had not invented bifocals and that no one else
who ever lived invented them either. Still, there might have existed
other people who don't in fact exist, and one of them might have
made the invention. In that case we *would have* used the description
'the inventor of bifocals' to refer to someone not among those who
actually have, do, or will exist. This is not to say that we actually *do*
refer to such a person, for there never have been and never will be
such people to refer to. Although it may be plausible to suppose that
we can refer to a merely possible person by the description 'the
person who would have existed if persons P and Q had conceived a
child at time t', there is no plausibility whatever in the notion that
'the person who would have existed if P and Q had conceived a child
at some time or other' uniquely picks out any possible person from all
the others. Why worry about the prospect of referring to merely
possible people when the plain truth seems to be this: descriptions
used referentially in the course of specifying a counterfactual situation refer to the objects which actually satisfy them (or at the very
least to the objects which the speaker thinks his audience believes
satisfies them). Otherwise they are not used referentially but attribu-

tively or ascriptively. For instance, if the definite description in (23) is used ascriptively then that sentence means simply

(25) If Jefferson had made Franklin's inventions he would have (uniquely) invented bifocals.

So the correct conclusion to draw from the fact that 'the inventor of bifocals' in (23) cannot refer to Franklin if (23) is to express a true proposition is not that it must refer to Jefferson, but that it does not refer to anyone at all.

These are the reasons why I think Kripke is mistaken, and the expressions 'one metre' and 'the length of S at t_0' can very well be synonymous. If at t_0 stick S had been shorter than it actually was, then the predicate 'one metre long' would have had a different extension and the description 'the length of S at t_0' would have referred to a different length, even though both expressions had possessed the same *sense* they do now and all other objects had retained their actual lengths. But S was not shorter than it was, and these expressions do not acquire different extensions or referents when used to describe counterfactual situations. Consider the sentence

(26) If at t_0 stick S had been shorter than it was, then the length which S had at t_0 would have been less than 39.37 inches.

If this is to express a true proposition, what can 'the length which S had at t_0' refer to? It cannot refer to the length one metre, i.e. 39.37 inches, since 39.37 inches could never have been greater or less than 39.37 inches. But there is a non-denumerable infinity of lesser lengths, and how could the description succeed in referring to just one of those lengths rather than to any other? The correct conclusion to draw is that the description does not refer to anything, and that (26) means nothing but

(27) If at t_0 stick S had been shorter than it was, then S would have had at t_0 a length less than 39.37 inches.

And obviously 'a length less than 39.37 inches' does not refer to a length less than 39.37 inches.

Let us now return to Harman's proposed counter-example to the Open Question Argument: water and H_2O. In front of me is a glass containing a colourless, odourless, tasteless liquid which I have collected from the kitchen tap and distilled to get rid of impurities. The liquid in the glass is chemically structured in some way or other, and the question arises: How is it chemically structured? Let us suppose that it is compose of H_2O molecules. And before relying on the existence of such Platonic entities as chemical structures over and above the things which are chemically structured, let us speak of the liquid in the glass being structured 'H_2O-wise' rather than having the structure H_2O, where to be structured H_2O-wise is to be composed of H_2O molecules. We may also identify the sample of liquid in the glass with a certain collection of elementary particles – electrons, protons, neutrons – which happen in this case to be arranged into H_2O molecules. Let us name this collection of particles 'the Sample'. I am going to define an artificial word 'WATER' in such a way that sentences of the form

(28)   x is WATER

mean simply

(29)   x is chemically structured as the Sample was at t_0.

Now although we are supposing that the Sample was structured H_2O-wise at t_0, it might not have been; the elementary particles of which it is composed might have arranged themselves into NH_3 molecules instead. In that case we would have had the same sample of liquid, but it would have been structured otherwise than it actually was, namely, NH_3-wise. Nevertheless, the sentence

(30)   The Sample was WATER at t_0

would still have expressed a necessary truth since it is synonymous with

(31)   At t_0 the Sample was structured as the Sample was structured at t_0.

And if these sentences had the same sense and reference which they actually have then they would express the same necessary truth which they now express. And then, although the Sample would *not* have been structured as it was, it would have been true that it *was* structured as it was. Or else, it would have been WATER no matter how it had been structured. The only way to avoid this consequence is to ensure that the necessary truth which (30) actually expresses is different from the one it would have expressed in the counter-factual situation; and this will be the case only if its sense or reference is different from what it would have been. Since there is no reason why the sense should change, it must be the reference that changes.

Following the treatment which I offered for the case of the metre stick I would suggest that, contrary to appearances, (31) does refer to something besides a sample of liquid and an instant of time; it refers to a chemical structure. The logical structure of (31) is better revealed by

(33)   At t_0 the Sample had the chemical structure which the Sample had at t_0.

Thus if the Sample had been composed of NH_3 molecules then (33) would have expressed a different tautology from the one it now expresses since 'the chemical structure which the Sample had at t_0' would have referred to a different structure. This is not the only way of ensuring that (31) would have had a different reference if the Sample had been composed of NH_3 molecules instead of H_2O molecules. We might suppose that when we say the Sample would not have been structured as it *actually* was, we are saying that it would not have been structured as it was in *the actual world*. If the Sample had been structured differently we still would have asserted a tautology by uttering the sentence

(34)   At t_0 the Sample was structured as the Sample was structured in the actual world at t_0.

But 'the actual world' would have referred to a different possible world from the one we actually use it to refer to. So we can ensure that if things had been otherwise (31) would have expressed a different truth, by virtue of referring either to different chemical structures or to different possible worlds.

I do not at the moment see what there is to choose between these two kinds of abstract entities, and if they serve equally well the purpose for which they have been introduced then a further problem arises. It is similar to the problem which faces set theory in identifying numbers with sets.[7] We might identify the number zero with the empty set, the number one with the set whose only member is zero, the number two with the set whose only members are zero and one, the number three with the set whose only members are zero, one, and two, etc. Or we might just as easily identify zero as before, one as before, but identify two with the set whose only member is one, and three with the set whose only member is two, etc. Neither system of identification is thought to be more correct than the other, and yet they have conflicting consequences; in one system three has more members than two, and in the other system they each have one member. This leads me to think that there is no reason to suppose that any identification of numbers with sets can be correct. And similarly, if it makes no difference whether we suppose sentences like (22) and (31) refer to lengths and structures rather than to possible worlds, then I can't see what could be making them refer to one rather than the other, in which case there would be no reason to suppose they refer to either. I can only hope that somewhere it does make a difference.

Before I leave this subject I should mention two final points. First, lengths were introduced in order to explain how the Standard Metre might have been less than a metre long even if 'The Standard Metre is a metre long' had expressed a true proposition. We explain it by saying that there exists a length which the Standard Metre might have had and which is *less than* the length which it did have. Of course, by 'less than' I cannot mean 'shorter than' or else the explanation will fall into an infinite regress similar to that which lies in wait for victims of the Third Man Argument: if in order for A to be shorter than B it is necessary that A should have a length which is shorter than the length of B, then these lengths themselves will be required to have lengths of which one is shorter than the other, etc. It is true that if length l_1 is *less* than length l_2 then they bear to each other the relation which ensures that objects which have l_1 are *shorter* than objects which have l_2; but what this relation is remains one of the mysteries of Platonism.

In the second place, I have argued that certain abstract objects must exist in order for our sentences to refer to them. But can't we refer to objects which don't exist?[8] When we say 'The great Library at Alexandria was destroyed by fire' we are surely talking about the great Library at Alexandria even though it no longer exists. And when I say 'My daughter Antigone will be a great scholar' am I not talking about my future daughter even though she doesn't yet exist? It may be conceded that it is possible to refer to objects that don't exist, as long as they either have existed or will exist. But can't we refer to the explosion that would have occurred if the time-bomb had not been defused? That explosion will not occur at any time, and yet we can even talk about the damage it would have caused, but didn't.

Perhaps it does make sense to talk of referring to things which never will exist but might have existed. However, abstract objects are not those sorts of things. If they don't exist, I can't imagine how they might have existed. For instance, symphonies might be considered abstract objects distinct from all the scores and performances which are merely their instantiations. Mozart's forty-second Symphony does not exist but it probably would have if he had lived longer; to that extent it makes sense to speak of referring to abstract objects which never existed but might have. But that is not the issue. The question is whether such activity as producing a concrete musical score might have resulted in the existence of an abstract symphony even if it does not. If it doesn't now, it is difficult to see under what other circumstances it would have. And that is why I think that abstract objects must actually exist if we are to refer to them.

Now Harman's counter-example concerned the ordinary word 'water', not my artificial word 'WATER', and it is great deal more complicated to explain how, in the ordinary sense of that word, the sentence 'Nothing can be water without being H_2O' expresses a true proposition. But any explanation that I have seen requires that we be able to refer to abstract entities such as chemical structures or possible worlds. If this is possible then Moore's Open Question Argument will not show that being water and being composed of H_2O molecules, or being yellow and reflecting light of a certain wavelength, are different properties which happen to be constantly conjoined. And if it is not a valid argument in Chemistry or Optics, why should it be a valid argument in Ethics? It appears that the validity of this argument will be determined only after more work has been done on the theory of reference.

ETHICAL PROPERTIES AND REAL ESSENCES

Knowing the sense of a descriptive expression is not always sufficient by itself to enable us to know the sorts of things to which it applies. It may be said that if the artificial word 'WATER' is defined as it was earlier, then in a sense we do know to which things it is applicable once we know the meaning of the word: we know it is correctly applied to things which are structured as a specified sample of liquid was structured at a given time. But which things are those? We will not know until we find out how the specified sample was structured at that time; and this requires empirical investigation. Without this extra information, knowing the sense of the word 'WATER' will not equip us to tell whether it can be correctly applied to anything not composed of H_2O molecules. But if the sense of the word does not by itself tell us the answer to this question at least it tells us what we have to find out in order to discover the answer. The sense of a descriptive expression does after all determine its extension, and by knowing its sense we know at least what we must find out in order to discover the extension.

If Naturalists wish to maintain that there are true, non-tautological definitions of the form 'To be a good X is the same as to be an X which is C', and seek to defend their position solely by appeal to synthetic statements asserting necessary identity and essentially involving some form of rigid designation, then the implication must be that the sense of evaluative expressions fixes their reference or extension in a way similar to that which is operative in the examples appealed to. Otherwise proper names, definite descriptions, and natural kind terms would not provide an analogical model by which to explain the alleged synthetic, real definitions of ethics.

But it is very implausible to suppose that evaluative terms function as, for instance, natural kind terms and have their extension fixed by their sense as the class of objects with certain properties whose description does *not* carry the same sense as the original evaluative terms themselves. It is not as though the ordinary, observable properties of actions, on the basis of which we commonly call them 'right' or 'wrong', merely accompany and serve to pick out the further underlying features which really make actions right or wrong. Diamonds, on the other hand, are the sorts of things whose overt appearance does not make them what they are. There can be immitation diamonds which are indistinguishable from the real thing to everyone but a few experts.[9] And people collected diamonds for thousands of years before it was discovered that to be a diamond was to be a certain crystal of carbon atoms. Milton meant precisely what we mean by the term 'diamond' and yet he had never heard of carbon atoms. The sense of the word specifies certain manifest properties, such as being a hard, clear, brilliant crystal, and it stipulates that to be a diamond is to have the underlying structure (whatever that turns out to be) which *actually* produces the characteristic appearance.

And it is often a long time before people are in a position to find out what this structure is. Even when it is discovered, it can generally be recognized only by a few people with specialized knowledge and elaborate equipment; the rest of us can easily be imposed upon by purveyors of immitations.

Could there be such a thing as an 'immitation' wrong action? That would have to be one that was indistinguishable from a genuine wrong action to all but a few moral experts. And until the underlying 'real essence' of wrongness was discovered it would be reasonable to suspect that what made actions wrong was not the properties in virtue of which we were accustomed to issue condemnations, nor any other property with which we were acquainted, but rather something which we had neither heard nor cared about. If there were two cases of causing gratuitous suffering solely for the amusement of the tormertor, and the cases were indistinguishable to anyone living, it would nevertheless be appropriate to wonder whether both actions had the right real essence; for if one of them didn't it would not really be wrong no matter how apparently similar it was to the other.

I think it is worth while at this point to examine an actual theory of ethical naturalism *de re* which has been advanced by R. M. Adams. In 'Divine Command Metaethics Modified Again'[10] he claims that moral wrongness is most plausibly identified with the property of being contrary to the commands of a loving God. He makes it clear that his claim does not constitute an ethical naturalism *de dicto*; i.e. an analysis of the meaning of the *word* 'wrong':

> Analysis of the concept or understanding with which the word 'wrong' is used is not sufficient to determine what wrongness is. What is can tell us about the nature of wrongness, I think, is that wrongness will be the property of actions (if there is one) that best fills the role assigned to wrongness by the concept. (p. 113.)

According to Adams the concept of wrongness is the concept of something which best satisfies such conditions as the following:

(i)   If possible, . . . the property to be identified with ethical wrongness should be one that actions have or lack objectively . . . independently of whether we think they do.

(ii) The property that is wrongness should belong to those types of action that are *thought* to be wrong – or at least it should belong to an important central group of them. [my emphasis]

(iii)   Wrongness should be a property that . . . plays a causal role
        (or a role as object of perception) in [wrong actions'] coming
        to be regarded as wrong. It should not be connected in a
        merely fortuitous way with our classification of actions as
        wrong or not wrong.

(iv)   Understanding the nature of wrongness should give one
        more rather than less reason to oppose wrong actions as
        such.

(v)   The best theory about the nature of wrongness should
        satisfy . . . [the] intuition that . . . rightness and wrongness
        are determined by a law or standard that has a sanctity that is
        greater than that of any merely human will or institution.
        (Ibid, p. 113)

There is one condition that is noticably absent from this list, a
condition which is almost paradigmatic of the concept of a natural
kind. The *real* essence of any natural kind is something which is
responsible for the manifest appearance of members of that kind.
Diamonds are hard, clear and brilliant *because* of their underlying
structure of carbon atoms. Elephants owe their characteristic appearance (a description of which specifies their *nominal* essence) to
their underlying genetic structure; and it is the possession of this
genetic structure that constitutes being an elephant. But the observable features of wrong actions are not due to God's forbidding such
actions. The causing of gratuitous suffering just for fun is something
which has all the *outward* characteristics of a wrong action; but no
one supposes that these features result from a further *hidden* property of such actions, viz. that they are forbidden by God. It is not
because they are forbidden by God that they have these properties;
on the contrary, it is because they have those properties that God
forbids them. So, on this theory, wrong actions do not form any sort
of natural kind, which is as it should be.

Condition (iv) does indeed seem to be part of the sense of the
word 'wrong', as prescriptivists have always claimed. But, if it is, it
precludes 'wrong' from having a naturalistic definition. In fact, condition (iv) is open to two interpretations, only one of which can be
regarded as specifying part of the sense of 'wrong'. This is the
interpretation according to which an action's having the property that
constitutes wrongness is a reason to oppose that action. Given that
interpretation, I would argue that it is not an objective (or even a
subjective) fact about an action that it is right or wrong, since to *call*

some feature a reason to oppose actions that have it is not to *state* any fact about that feature. It is to issue a prescription which means: 'Other things being equal, oppose such actions because they have that property' (see Chapter 3, above). Thinking that an action A is wrong will then partly consist in sincerely assenting to the prescription: 'There is some property p, such that (other things being equal) oppose action A since it has p.' To say why action A is wrong is to say which property p is.

According to the other interpretation of condition (iv), it says that our awareness of this feature must motivate us to some extent to oppose actions which have it; it must be a feature that people will care about once they discover what it is. So, any feature which people will not in fact care about when they become aware of it is disqualified as a candidate for moral wrongness. But why couldn't the fault lie with us who do not care, rather than with the feature we do not care about? A prescriptivist would be the first to admit that he would not *call* an action wrong if he were not motivated by any of its features to oppose it; but he would insist that it may nevertheless *be* wrong even if he is so depraved that he doesn't care about it. Surely there are plenty of people who will not care: if the Gestapo torturer is not moved even by the suffering of his victims, it is not likely that anything else (which could plausibly be identified with wrongness) will move him. Adams writes:

> Because of what is believed about God's actions, purposes, character, and power, he inspires such devotion and/or fear that contrariness to his commands is seen as a supremely weighty reason for opposing an action (Ibid., p. 115.)

The fear inspired is presumably the fear of post-mortem punishment for those who break God's commandments. But this raises two problems. First, the problem of evil: what reason could there be to say that God is a loving God if he permits criminals a free rein on earth and punishes them after death only to make them 'pay' for their crimes and not to change their character? Such a God obviously thinks it is better to have both the crime and the punishment than to have neither if that requires interfering with the freedom of the criminal. We, of course, disagree with such a God, or else we would not spend so much money in support of the police force whose job it is to prevent crime from occurring and not just to catch the criminals after the fact. This shows that we have a higher regard for the safety of the criminal's intended victim than for the free-will of the criminal. The problem this poses for Adams' version of ethical naturalism is as follows: necessarily, if any being is a loving God then he wants what is best for his creatures; therefore, in order to determine whether any being claiming to be a loving God really is who he says he is, we must decide whether what he wants for us really is best; and unless we can give a naturalistic definition of 'what is best for us' (apart from just 'whatever a loving God happens to want for us') then contrareity to the commands of a loving God will not constitute a naturalistic definition of moral wrongness.[11] Relying on my own notions of what is best for us I would conclude that a loving God would not inflict post-mortem punishments on anyone since they will not do any good; consequently, criminals have nothing to fear from a loving God, if there is one.

The second problem raised by the motive of fear is that awareness of the property identical with wrongness was supposed to motivate us to oppose wrong actions 'as such'. And I would not have expected that opposing wrong actions 'as such' should be the same as opposing them out of fear of punishment. It has traditionally, but perhaps mistakenly, been thought that to refrain from wrongdoing out of fear of punishment is to be motivated by extraneous considerations and not by an awareness of the action's wrongness 'as such'. Some writers appear to hold that tradition is mistaken on this point. Consider Hobbes:

> But this difficulty of obeying both God, and the Civill Soveraign on earth, to those that can distinguish between what is *Necessary*, and what is not *Necessary* for their *Reception* into the *Kingdome of God*, is of no moment. For if the command of the Civill Soveraign bee such, as that it may be obeyed, without the forfeiture of life Eternall; not to obey it is unjust; . . . But if the command be such, as cannot be obeyed, without being damned to Eternall Death, then it were madnesse to obey it, and the Counsell of our Saviour takes place, (Mat. 10. 28) 'Fear not those that kill the body, but cannot kill the soule'. (*Leviathan*, ch. 43. para. 2.)

The prudent course of action is obviously to obey the most fearsome authority; and prudence may, surprisingly, be what morality comes down to. Geach, echoing Hobbes, writes:

> But what if somebody asks 'Why should I obey God's Law?'. This is really an insane question [since a] defiance of an Almighty God is

insane: . . I shall be told . . . that since I am saying not: It is your supreme moral duty to obey God, but simply: It is insane to set about defying an Almighty God, my attitude is plain power worship. But since this is worship of the Supreme Power, it is as such wholly different from, and does not carry with it, a cringing attitude towards earthly powers. An earthly potentate does not compete with God, even unsuccessfully: he may threaten all manner of afflictions, but only from God's hands can any affliction actually come upon us. ('The Moral Law and the Law of God' in *God and the Soul*, Routledge & Kegan Paul, 1969, pp. 126–7.)

In Hobbes' view it is God's infinite power that makes it wrong to disobey him (cf. *Leviathan*, ch. 31, paras 5–7). And if he is right then fear is not an extraneous motive. But in Adams' view it is supposed to be God's love that makes disobedience wrong, in which case opposing wrong actions 'as such' is different from opposing them out of the fear.

This brings us to devotion. And here the difficulty is that no God will inspire devotion in his followers unless he is believed to be good and his actions are thought to be right. If he does not at least appear to be good then he may inspire fear but never devotion. But in order to *appear* good and just, he must achieve a high score on *our* tests for right and wrong, which consequently must embody a standard independent of his commands and capable of judging their validity. (This is not to say that our standards are the correct ones just because they are ours, but obviously they are the only ones *we* have.) Even Adams must admit this, for he writes:

'It is contrary to God's commands to do X' implies 'It is wrong to do X' only if certain conditions are assumed – namely, only if it is assumed that God has the character which I believe him to have, of loving his human creatures. If God were really to command us to make cruelty our goal, then he would not have that character of loving us, and I would not say it would be wrong to disobey him. ('A Modified Divine Command Theory of Ethical Wrongness'; repr. in Helm (ed.:), *Divine Commands and Morality*, p. 86).

And if we can know independently that a loving God would *not* command cruelty for its own sake, then presumably we can know just as independently what a loving God *would* command. Then it is hard to see why there must actually be such a God at all. Why wouldn't

Adams be satisfied with the claim that 'X is morally wrong' means 'X *would* be contrary to the commands of a loving God if there *were* one'? Then he would not have to say that no actions are morally wrong if there *is* no loving God.

The same problem assails condition (v), of which Adams writes:

> God's commands constitute a law or standard that seems to be-
> lievers to have a sanctity that is not possessed by any merely human
> will or institution. (op. cit., p. 115).

If God's law has any sanctity it is because of *what* it commands, not who commands it. The only way we have to identify which law has sanctity, and consequently whose law is to count as God's law, is to examine the content of the law, not its source. Even if there were an independent way of identifying the source we would still have to examine the content according to our own standards in order to determine whether this source is a loving God or merely a powerful God. And to do this we must decide whether what the law commands is for the best. So once more, unless we have a naturalistic definition of 'good' we lack one for 'wrong'.

Condition (iii) requires that it be no accident that the actions we classify as wrong have the property which, unknown to us, constitutes wrongness. And according to Adams, contrariety to the laws of a loving God 'plays a causal role in our classification of actions as wrong, in so far as God has created our moral faculties to reflect his commands' (p. 115). I take this to mean that God might have created our moral faculties differently but in fact chose to create them so that the observable properties of those actions which he forbids will cause us to experience certain *feelings* (of 'disapprobation', as Hume calls them). And as a result of having these feelings we think of those actions as being wrong. Now we might also think that God created our faculty of visual perception in such a way that objects which reflect a certain kind of light into our eyes cause us to have a particular sort of visual experience. And we have set aside the word 'red' as the name of the class of objects which have the power to cause that sort of experience in perceivers like us (should there be any). God might have created our visual faculties differently, so that those objects caused in us a different experience. Even so, we might have used the word 'red' of the same class of objects, and meant the same thing by it. The power that enables those objects to cause one kind of experience in perceivers like us is the same power that enables them to cause different experiences in different perceivers; so the power we attributed to such objects by calling them red would be the same no matter what kind of experience they caused us to have.

No one thinks, however, that there is a right or wrong kind of experience for red objects to cause; there is nothing in nature that makes a given experience appropriate or inappropriate to be caused by light of a particular wave-length; any other kind of visual experience would have been just as appropriate. People whose visual spectrum is inverted are not worse off, or mistaken, just different. But that is not how we think of our moral feelings. Revulsion and outrage are appropriate reactions to the slaughter of innocent, unarmed civilians but not to the self-sacrificing rescue of innocents in distress. Since our moral emotions can be either fitting or unfitting reactions to particular actions, it makes sense to ask whether God matched the actions and our reactions *appropriately*, while it makes no sense to ask whether he matched our visual experiences to light-waves appropriately. It does not seem sufficient to say merely that he matched them fittingly because he matched them as he saw fit; even a God who was not loving could have done that much. If matchings are to be appropriate or inappropriate there must be a standard of appropriateness against which God's matchings can count as fitting or unfitting, suitable or unsuitable; otherwise, any way which God chose to match them would have been just as appropriate as any other way he might have chosen. The standard, of course, is that according to which a *loving* God would match our emotions, although, by choosing to create our moral faculties as he did, God has fixed in advance which standard we take this to be. So we have a dilemma: either there is an independent standard which God must adhere to if his matchings are to be appropriate, but it is God's good pleasure that determines which standard we think this is; or there is no independent standard, in which case his matchings cannot be either appropriate or inappropriate.

In other words; our ideas of morality, if this account is right, have the same origin with our ideas of the sensible qualities of bodies, the harmony of sounds, or the beauties of painting or sculpture; that is, the mere good pleasure of our Maker adapting the mind and its organs in a particular manner to certain objects. Virtue (as those who embrace this scheme say) is an affair of taste . . . Our perception of *right*, or moral good, in actions, is that agreeable *emotion*, or feeling, which certain actions produce in us; and of

wrong, or moral evil, the contrary. They are particular modifica-
tions of our minds, or impressions which they are made to receive
from the contemplation of certain actions, which the contrary
actions *might* have occasioned, had the Author of nature so
pleased. Richard Price, *A Review of the Principle Questions in
Morals*, 3rd edn 1787, ed. D. D. Raphael, OU. P, 1974, pp.
14–15.)

These are the sorts of problems that plague any theory of the divine
origin of the moral sense.[12]

It seems to me that Adams' Divine Command theory does not
provide a successful ethical naturalism *de re*; furthermore *any* attempt to provide one will be aborted by condition (iv). If this
condition really does specify part of the sense of 'wrong' then it
cannot be a fact about any action that it is wrong, since it is not a fact
about any property that an action's having it is a reason to refrain
from that action. (This, of course, is *not* to say that actions cannot be
wrong or that an action's having a certain property cannot be a
reason not to do it.) On the other hand, if it is not part of the sense of
'wrong' that the wrongness of an action is a reason not to do it, then
ethical naturalism will be a 'so what?' morality: it will be possible for
people consistently to think that although a certain action is wrong
yet this provides no reason whatever to refrain from doing it.[13]

5 Subjectivity and Objectivity

DISPOSITIONS AND BUILT-IN PRESCRIPTIVITY

Inevitably some readers will be dissatisfied unless value judgements, and especially moral judgements, are given an interpretation which makes them capable of being objectively true or false. Such readers wish to be assured that when they call an action morally wrong they are stating an objective fact about it, if indeed the action is wrong. Now there is no lack of empirical facts which we might discover and communicate, and it might be thought that we need only ask the 'objectivists' which of these facts they intend that moral judgements should state. After all, it is only because of the contingent linguistic fact that a given sentence means what it does that it is used to express one particular proposition rather than some other, and if there is no disagreement concerning any of the empirical facts about an action then it seems petty to maintain a dispute over the words which are to be used to express those facts. As long as I am able to say everything I wish to say about an action, it makes no difference to me whether I am to use one set of noises instead of another to say those things; a decision to use a word with one meaning rather than another affects only the way I talk about actions, not the way I think about them. Unfortunately, most of the people who wish moral judgements to state objective facts do not intend that they should state any of the familiar empirical facts which we can establish about actions. And this is because they also wish moral judgements to be intrinsically action-guiding whereas judgements of empirical fact are only contingently action-guiding; for example, sadistic torturers are just as aware of the suffering of their victims as anyone else would be, and yet this awareness does not make them desist although it would make others try to get them to desist.

What seems to be desired is a realm of 'objective values' about which there would be, for instance, objective moral facts which are

139

nevertheless non-empirical and yet non-tautological facts and such that mere awareness of them necessarily causes people to pursue what has objective value if they are able. But such a desire is incoherent. Consider J. L. Mackie's characterization of this supposed realm.

> Plato's Forms give a dramatic picture of what objective values would have to be. The Form of the Good is such that knowledge of it provides the knower with both a direction and an overriding motive; something's being good both tells the person who knows this to pursue it and makes him pursue it. An objective good would be sought by anyone who was acquainted with it, not because of any contingent fact that this person, or every person, is so constituted that he desires this end, but just because the end has to-be-pursuedness somehow built into it. Similarly, if there were objective principles of right and wrong, any wrong (possible) course of action would have not-to-be-doneness somehow built into it. *Ethics: Inventing Right and Wrong*, Penguin 1977, p. 40.)

Now what does it *mean* to say that a goal or purpose has 'to-be-pursuedness' built into it? Suppose someone were to say that God has to-be-obeyedness somehow built into him. I can only understand this to mean that part of *saying* that some being is God is to say that he is to be obeyed, so that 'X is God' logically entails 'Obey X.' But then it would follow that no judgement of the form 'X is God' could ever be true, since, on any plausible theory of entailment, the truth of 'X is God' logically prevents it from entailing 'Obey X.' According to one theory, if 'X is God' were true and entailed 'Obey X', then 'Obey X' would be true as well; but since 'Obey X' is a prescription and is incapable of being true or false, it follows that 'X is God' cannot both be true and entail 'Obey X.' It would be very unpromising to suggest that 'X is God' entails 'Obey X' if it is logically impossible that the former be true and the latter be false. For although it is impossible for 'Obey X' to be false, the same can be said for 'Disobey X', so that on this suggestion 'X is God' will entail both 'Obey X' and 'Disobey X'; in fact, any statement of fact will logically entail any prescription whatever. In the logic of satisfaction, on the other hand, the statement 'X is God' entails the prescription 'Obey X' only if it is logically impossible for the statement to be true and the prescription to go unfulfilled; but since it is not logically impossible to disobey God, it follows again that if 'X is God' were a true statement it could never entail 'Obey X.' Similarly, if someone were to say that happiness is a goal that has to-be-pursuedness built into it, I could only understand this to mean that part of what it is to *call* a situation a happy one in certain respects is to say that such situations are to be pursued, so that 'S is a happy situation' entails 'pursue situations like S'. But once more, this would prevent it from being *true* that any situation was a happy one to be in. So the price to be paid for buildng to-be-pursuedness into a goal, i.e. for building the prescription to pursue that goal into the very description of the goal, is that it could never be true or false (objectively or otherwise) that any goal fit that 'description'.

This interpretation seems, in fact, to be what Mackie has in mind. When he attributes to objectivists the view that wrong actions have not-to-be-doneness built into them, he appears to be speaking of the view that the *judgement* that an action is wrong has built into it the *prescription* that it not be done, so that 'Action A is wrong' entails 'Don't do A.' He says that when the ordinary person calls an action wrong he wishes to be saying something about the action as it is in itself, and not merely to be expressing his own attitudes or feelings:

> But the something he wants to say is not purely descriptive, certainly not inert, but something that involves a call for action or for the refraining from action, and one that is absolute, not contingent upon any desire or preference or policy or choice, his own or anyone else's. (Ibid., p. 33)

And yet how can a call for action be true or false? I understand how 'Alons, alons aux barricades' is a call for action, but it is not a statement that is either true or false. On the other hand, it may be true that 'England expects every man to do his duty' but this is not a call to action; being reminded of its truth might motivate some people to action, but only those who already care about England. What is required is a fact that will motivate everyone who is aware of it to pursue the same value, no matter what his desires or concerns happen to be.

In Plato's theory the Forms, and in particular the Form of the Good, are eternal, extra-mental, realities. They are a very central structural element in the fabric of the world. But it is held also that just knowing them or 'seeing' them will not merely tell men what to do but will ensure that they do it, overruling any contrary inclinations. The philosopher-kings in the *Republic* can, Plato thinks, be trusted with unchecked power because their education will have given them knowledge of the Forms. Being acquainted with the Forms of the Good and Justice and Beauty and the rest they will, by this knowledge alone, without any further motivation, be impelled to pursue and promote these ideals. (Ibid., pp. 23–4)

Now much of what is said here about awareness of the Forms can be applied to jumping off of cliffs or out of windows. For instance, merely jumping out of a window will not only show me the ground below, but will ensure that I go there, overruling any contrary inclination; having jumped out of the window I will, by this action alone, without any further motivation, be impelled toward the ground. We do not suppose it is a mere coincidence that, in certain familiar circumstances, objects which are left unsupported always fall toward the ground; rather, we postulate a *disposition* to fall, and set physicists to work discovering its underlying physical basis. That is, we think there is a reason why things fall and we try to find out what it is. Having a disposition to fall is certainly distinct from actually falling or being left unsupported, and if only we knew what this disposition was then we could explain why unsupported objects fall. But even if there is such a disposition, this is only a contingent fact about the nature of matter; that is, either the matter which presently exists might not have had this disposition, or else, if it could not have lacked this disposition and continued to exist, it might never have existed and the universe might have contained a different sort of matter in its place. Similarly, if it is not to be a mere coincidence that people who are aware of the Forms always pursue the relevant ideals, then such people must have a *disposition* to pursue those ideals when they are aware of the Forms just as they have a disposition to fall downward when they jump out of windows. It is easy to give names to these unknown dispositions; the disposition to fall when left unsupported near the surface of the earth is called 'gravitational mass', and the disposition to behave in a certain way upon acquiring a factual belief is what I call a 'desire'. And it is obvious that merely giving names to these dispositions does nothing to advance our understanding of why people behave the way they do when they acquire factual beliefs or jump out of windows. Nevertheless, without those dispositions their behaviour would be purely coincidental: it would never be true that a person fell to the ground *because* he jumped out of a window, or that he pursued a certain ideal *because* he became aware of some Platonic Form. And it is a contingent fact that people are so constructed as to have such dispositions. The tendency to pursue an ideal when acquainted with a Platonic Form is something which is distinct from actually pursuing that ideal or actually being acquainted with the Form; not only can one have the tendency without ever being acquainted with the Forms or pursuing the ideals, it is also logically possible to have the knowledge and, as a matter of pure coincidence, pursue the ideals without having any tendency to do so upon 'seeing' the Forms (just as there is no inconsistency in the idea that objects with no gravitational mass should always fall downward for no reason at all when released near the surface of the earth).

By interpreting desires as nothing but dispositions to behave in various ways upon the fulfillment of certain antecedent conditions, I have ensured that the theory of 'objective prescriptions' which Mackie attacks is logically inconsistent, and not, as he takes it to be, coherent but highly implausible.

> The objective values which I am denying would be action-directing absolutely, not contingently (in the way indicated upon the agent's desires and inclinations. (Ibid., p. 29)

For a fact to be 'intrinsically action-guiding' is simply for people who are capable of becoming aware of this fact to possess a disposition to pursue a certain goal once they do become aware of it. Consequently it is logically impossible for there to be facts which are capable of motivating certain behaviour in people who are aware of them no matter what dispositions these people have; for the presence of the relevant disposition is logically necessary if awareness of these facts is to *motivate* (rather then merely precede) such behaviour. And it must be remembered that by assigning to desires the status of dispositions I do not trivialize this claim; for, as I argued in Chapter 3, desires are *distinct* from beliefs and are required if beliefs are to motivate action, even though we contribute nothing toward the *explanation* of action if we refer to these desires simply as 'dispositions'.

RELIGION

After expounding the 'Argument from Relativity' and the 'Argument from Queerness' in order to make objective prescriptivism appear to be a very implausible ethical theory, Mackie makes a rather surprising concession. ´

> To meet these difficulties, the objectivist may have recourse to the purpose of God: the true purpose of human life is fixed by what God intended (or, intends) men to do and to be. Actual human strivings and satisfactions have some relation to this true end because God made men for this end and made them such as to pursue it – but only *some* relation, because of the inevitable imperfection of created beings.
>
> I concede that if the requisite theological doctrine could be defended, a kind of objective ethical prescriptivity could be thus introduced. Since I think that theism cannot be defended, I do not regard this as any threat to my argument. (Ibid., p. 48)

It is difficult to see how *any* kind of objective prescriptivity would be established by the truth of this theological doctrine. In the first place, awareness of certain alleged ethical facts would impell us to pursue and promote the true end of human life only because of the utterly contingent fact that 'God made men for this end and made them such as to pursue it.' Obviously he might have made us differently, and endowed us with different desires and inclinations. He might, for instance, have made us more benevolent and sympathetic. But the theory of objective prescriptivity requires that awareness of ethical facts should motivate people to pursue the true end of human life no matter what desires they happen to be endowed with, i.e.

> not because of any contingent fact that this person, or every person, is so constituted that he desires this end, but just because the end has to-be-pursuedness somehow built into it. (Ibid., p. 40)

It is one thing for God to build into our nature a desire to pursue a certain end, but it is something else (if indeed it is anyting at all) for God to build into the end itself a feature called 'to-be-pursuedness'.

In the second place, no mere fact about what goal we were created to pursue will ever logically entail a prescription to pursue that goal. Consider what is involved in answering a question such as 'What is the meaning or purpose of life?.' It is sometimes said that if life has no meaning then it does not really matter what we do. And in a sense this is true, if all we *mean* by saying that life is not meaningless is that it does matter what we do with our lives. But often people who talk of the meaning of life have something quite different in mind. To put it crudely, they want to know that we were put on this earth to do. Yet even if no one put us here to do anything, it would be a mistake to conclude that it does not matter what we do now that we are here. The claim that no one put us here for any reason has no necessary bearing at all on the question what to do while we are here. For it may still be important to pursue a certain goal even if no one put us here to pursue it.

To see that our having been created for a purpose is not sufficient to provide an answer to the question what to do with our lives, imagine that Satan created us and put us on the earth to torment one another and thereby provide him with a source of endless amusement. In that case there would be a perfectly adequate answer to the factual question 'For what purpose were we created?' but not one that logically entailed any answer to the practical question what to do now that we are alive. Someone could say quite appropriately 'I know that we were put here to make life miserable for each other, but why do what we were put here to do?.' To discover that we were put here to do something is one thing, to decide to do it is quite another. And this is true no matter what we were put here to do. As long as the possibility of devoting our lives to some particular end does not depend on our being created for that end, we can decide to pursue that goal evel if we were not put here to pursue it or were put here to pursue some other goal.

'But God's purpose for us is a good one, and therefore we ought to promote it.' This is simply a consequence of the definition of the word 'God', since nothing could merit the title of 'God' if its purposes were not good. Obviously, if part of saying 'To do X is God's purpose for us' is saying 'To do X is the purpose for us of a being whose purposes are to be pursued' then the claim that God's purpose for us is that we pursue a certain goal will logically entail the prescription to pursue that goal. But then the claim will not be capable of being true, and we would first have to decide whether to further that purpose before we could decide whether the being who had this purpose for us was really God.[1]

'WHAT MATTERS?'

People are concerned about different things; one thing matters to one person, another thing to someone else. But apart from knowing that something matters to one person and does not matter to another, we can also ask whether anything matters 'in itself' independently of its mattering to anyone. We also say that whatever anyone believes is (by definition) true for him, and wonder whether there is anything which is simply true independently of anyone believing it. The analogy tempts us to suspect that truth bears a relation to belief which is similar to a relation which importance bears to concern: just as our belief is misplaced if what we beleive is not true, so our concern is misplaced if what we care about does not really matter.

Nothing is more common than to hear it said that some people care most about things of little importance, such as wealth and reputation. We even say of ourselves that we used to be concerned about things which we now recognize to be trivial and unimportant, and this leads us to wonder whether we might not simply have switched our concern from one triviality to another. Perhaps no one has ever succeeded in caring for something that matters; after all, we admit this to be the case with other people and even with ourselves at other times. Of course I cannot sincerely admit of any particular object of concern that it *does* not matter without at the same time ceasing to care about it, just as I cannot admit that a particular belief of mine *is* false without giving up my belief in it. But this does not stop me from suspecting that something I care about *may* not matter any more than it prevents me from thinking that such-and-such a belief of mine *may* not be true. In fact, I am certain that somewhere among my beliefs there is at least one which actually *is* false; I just don't know where it is and consequently don't know which to abandon. The same holds for my concerns.

But not only are we led to conjecture that there is something which matters although no one cares about it (because they are busy caring about other things that don't matter), the doubt also arises that perhaps we are busy worrying about these things when nothing really matters at all. In that case the tautology that one should care only about what matters would show that all our concerns were misplaced and inappropriate and that we should not care about anything. And of course we could not come to believe that nothing matters without at the same time ceasing to care about things.

Now it is sometimes suggested that to say that to say we might be mistaken in thinking some particular object of concern to be important is merely to say that we might change our minds about it and cease to be concerned with or think it important. And since the possibility that we should come to lose concern for absolutely everything is very remote, so is the possibility that nothing should really matter. But it seems to me false that the possibility of being mistaken amounts simply to the possibility of changing our minds. Certainly my *being* mistaken in thinking something to be important is simply my thinking it to be important when it is not. And this is not the same as my coming to change my mind at some time in the future; for a mere change of mind could easily be a shift of concern from something that matters to something trivial, in which case I would be mistaken after the change rather than before it. I cannot accept that *your* ceasing to think something important implies that *you* were mistaken to begin with; for that would commit me to holding that you once thought it was important when it was *not*, and I cannot agree that it was not important without *myself* not caring about it. For the same reason I am hardly going to admit that my ceasing to think something important shows that I was mistaken to care about it (all it shows is that I will *think* I was mistaken to care about it). And if my *being* mistaken is not the same as my coming to change my mind, then the *possibility* of my being mistaken cannot be identical with the possibility of my coming to change my mind.

What then does it mean to say that what we think to be important might not really be important? We cannot answer this question until we have some idea what it is to say or think that something *is* important. Hare's view, which I endorse, is that to think something to be important is simply to care about it, and that

> when we say something matters or is important what we are doing, in saying this, is to express concern about that something. . . . To be concerned about something is to be disposed to make certain choices, certain efforts, in the attempt to affect in some way that about which we are concerned. '"Nothing Matters"' in R. M. Hare, *Applications of Moral Philosophy*, pp. 33–4, 36.)

To *think* that something matters is to be concerned about it, which is to have a complex disposition to do various things under different circumstances. To *say* that something matters or is important is to say that it is something to be concerned about, which is to issue a prescription to care about it. To ask why it is important is to ask 'Why care about it?', where the answer will point out a reason for caring about it and can therefore be expressed in the form of a prescription: 'Care about it because . . .'.

And this provides a solution to the question of what our fallibility consists in or what it *means* to say that we might be mistaken about what matters. If we say that a certain thing is important then we are either right or wrong, although what we say is neither true nor false. What we say, when we claim a thing to be important, is *right* just in case some fact constitutes an overriding reason to care about that thing;[2] by saying what that fact is we answer the question 'What makes your claim right?.' If we are asked 'What makes that fact a reason?' we would have to reply: 'Because of the fact that P is true, be concerned about X since it is a fact that Q is true', and so on indefinitely for any further questions that may be raised. To say that the claim 'X is important' is wrong is to say that there is no fact which constitutes a reason to be concerned about X, which is the same as to say that the claim 'X is not important' is right. This brings us to fallibility. If we are using sentences of the form 'X matters' and 'X is important' prescriptively, then to say that *we might be mistaken* about what matters is to say that *there might be no reason* to care about some of the things we actually do care about.

It may be said that this is a subjectivist account of what it is to say that something matters, but it is not clear what such a charge would amount to. It is clearly a prescriptivist account and not a descriptivist one: to say that something matters is not to state any fact about it, objective or subjective, although it is to prescribe concern for it because of some objective property it has. So, in addition to the subjective concern which people feel for different things there are innumerable objective properties which characterize those things. But none of them is the property of mattering. The reason is that acknowledging an objective property of things does not logically commit anyone to care about things that have it, since no statement of fact describing a thing can entail any prescription to care about it. However, the judgement that a thing matters does entail such a prescription, and so there must be a prescriptive element in the judgement of importance which is lacking in the statement of fact.

Hare has argued that it makes no difference to the importance of anything that values are not "built into the fabric of the universe", since there are still the same things to care about and the same reasons for caring about them. In a famous passage he asks that we

think of one world into whose fabric values are objectively built; and think of another in which those values have been annihilated. And remember that in both worlds the people in them go on being concerned about the same things – there is no difference in the 'subjective' concern which people have for things, only in their 'objective' value. Now I ask, what is the difference between the states of affairs in these two worlds? Can any other answer be given except 'None whatever'? ('"Nothing Matters"', p. 47)

Mackie has a comment on this passage which is worth quoting in full.

Now it is quite true that it is logically possible that the subjective concern, the activity of valuing or of thinking things wrong, should go on in just the same way whether there are objective values or not. But to say this is only to reiterate that there is a logical distinction between first and second order ethics: first order judgements are not necessarily affected by the truth or falsity of a second order view. But it does not follow, and it is not true, that there is no difference whatever between these two worlds. In the one there is something which backs up and validates some of the subjective concern which people have for things, and in the other there is not. Hare's argument is similar to the positivist claim that there is no difference between a phenomenalist or Berkeleian world in which there are only minds and their ideas and the common sense realist one in which there are also material things, because it is logically possible that people should have the same experiences in both. If we reject the positivism that would make the dispute between realists and phenominalists a pseudo-question, we can reject Hare's similarly supported dismissal of the issue of the objectivity of values. (*Ethics: Inventing Right and Wrong*; pp. 21–2.)

My objection to Mackie's reply is this: whatever it is that 'backs up and validates some of the subjective concern which people have for things' in a world containing the supposed objective values will also back up and validate the same concern which people would have in a world without objective values. Some people are concerned about the fact that thousands of political prisoners in many countries are being tortured and millions of people throughout the world are starving to death. What justifies and *validates* this concern is simply the fact that torture and starvation cause immense suffering; and they would still cause immense suffering even if there were no such things as objective values. Mackie would have to maintain that the suffering involved in torture and starvation validates our concern about those evils only in a world containing objective values that can somehow secure this relation of validation. But there is no such relation to secure or fail to secure. When we say that the suffering of the victims justifies or validates our concern for them we are not stating any fact about their suffering or our concern: we are not, for instance, stating that their suffering stands in the relation 'validates' to our concern. What I, for one, am doing is expressing a kind of universalizable *wish* which resolves into an idle wish and an active desire; that is, the expression of this wish entails imperative sentences in some of the persons and some of the tenses, and optative sentences in the rest of the persons and tenses. It entails, for instance, 'Because of their suffering, be concerned for them' and 'Because of their suffering, would that others had been concerned for them.' If someone were to say 'Why concern yourself with these people? After all, there are no objective values', a perfectly adequate response would be 'Concern yourself with these people because they are suffering.' The existence or non-existence of objective values has no bearing whatever on the question we address when we try to *decide* what to care about; and as a logical consequence of this, don't let the status of objective values bear in any way on that decision.

Notes

1 THE RELEVANCE OF MORALITY TO PRACTICE

1. 'Ethical Intuitionism' *Philosophy*, vol. 24, 1949, see pp. 26–7.
2. See W. D. Ross. *Foundations of Ethics*, OUP, 1939, p. 168; H. A. Prichard: 'Does Moral Philosophy Rest on a Mistake?' in *Moral Obligation*, OUP, 1968, pp. 7–8.
3. H. A. Prichard, 'Does Moral Philosophy Rest on a Mistake?', p. 8.
4. *A Review of the Principal Questions in Morals*, 3rd ed, 1787; ed. D. D. Raphael, OUP, 1974, pp. 25–7.
5. Compare J. L. Mackie, *Problems from Locke*, OUP, 1976, pp. 215–22.
6. Cf. John Wisdon, 'Metaphysics and Verification' in *Philosophy and Psychoanalysis*, Blackwell, 1953, pp. 95–9.
7. See Nicholas P. White, 'Inquiry', vol. XXVIII, 1974.
8. See e.g. *Freedom and Reason*, OUP, 1963, ch. 2, esp. p. 9; 'The Argument from Received Opinion' in *Essays on Philosophical Method*, Macmillan, 1971, esp. pp. 119–20.
9. For a similar argument to the effect that conclusion (3) above is the important claim, and not whether (1) or (2) can be denied without contradiction, see Peter Singer: 'The Triviality of the Debate Over "Is-Ought" and the Definition of "Moral" ', *American Philosophical Quarterly*, vol. 10, 1973.
10. This example, with only slight modification, was taken from Hare, 'The Argument from Received Opinion', p. 124.

2 SOME ASPECTS OF THE LOGIC OF PRESCRIPTIONS

1. 'A Doubt about Universal Prescriptivism', *Analysis* vol. 39, no. 3, 1979.
2. See e.g. A. P. French, *Vibrations and Waves*, W. W. Norton & Co., 1971, pp. 7–10.
3. In A. I. Goldman and J. Kim (eds), *Values and Morals*, Reidel, 1978.
4. G. E. M. Anscombe, *Intention*, 2nd ed, Blackwell, 1963.
5. B. A. O. Williams, 'Imperative Inference', *Analysis*, supplementary vol., 1963.
6. In 'Some Alleged Differences Between Imperatives and Indicatives', repr. in *Practical Inferences*, Macmillan, 1972.
7. *Analysis*, vol. 18, 1957–8; reprinted in Geach's *Logic Matters*, Blackwell, 1972 (reference is to the latter).

8. *Philosophy*, vol. 52, 1977.
9. Ibid.
10. 'The Runabout Inference Ticket', *Analysis*, vol. 21, 1960.
11. 'Abstract Objects', *Review of Metaphysics*, vol. XVI, 1964.

3   A REASON TO DO SOMETHING

1. In 'Descriptivism', repr. in *Essays on the Moral Concepts*, University of California Press, 1972, pp. 73–4.
2. Cf. John McDowell, 'Are Moral Requirements Hypothetical Imperatives?', *PASS*, vol. LII, 1978: 'Virtue and Reason,' *The Monist*, vol. 62, 1979: also Thomas Nagel, *The Possibility of Altruism*, OUP, 1970. Both writers are defending Kant's views on the role of inclinations in virtuous motivation as expounded in the *Groundwork to the Metaphysics of Morals*.
3. I. G. McFetridge offers this example in his contribution to the symposium 'Are Moral Requirements Hypothetical Imperatives'; *PASS*, vol. LII, 1978, p. 36.
4. In 'Ethical Intuitionism', *Philosophy*, vol. 24, 1949; see Chapter 1 above, pp. 1–6.
5. *The Nature of Morality*, OUP, 1977, esp. pp. 83–90, 'Moral Relativism Defended'; *The Philosophical Review*, vol. LXXXIV, 1975, 'What Is Moral Relativism'; in A. I. Goldman and J. Kim (eds), *Values and Morals*, Reidel, 1978.
6. 'Moore's Arguments against Certain Forms of Ethical Naturalism', in P. A. Schilpp (ed.), *The Philosophy of G. E. Moore*, Open Court, 1942 (3rd ed, 1968, p. 82).
7. This example comes from Barry Barnes and David Bloor: 'Relativism, Rationalism and the Sociology of Knowledge' in M. Hollis and S. Lukes (eds), *Rationality and Relativism*, Blackwell, 1982. Criticizing Ryle's view that a causal explanation is required for our mental performances only when these performances go wrong, they write: 'Perhaps one day the dualist account of Ryle and Hamlyn will be developed into its ultimate form, and we will be told that the operations of adding machines are causally determined only when erroneous results are produced, and that at other times such machines operate rationally in ways which require no explanation.' (p. 33, footnote).
8. For a Wittgensteinian attempt to expose the Problem of Induction as a misuse of the term 'reason', see Paul Edwards, 'Bertrand Russell's Doubts About Induction'; *Mind*, 1949, repr. in A. G. N. Flew (ed.) *Logic and Language: First Series*, Blackwell, 1951.

4   ETHICAL NATURALISM *DE RE*

1. See, for example, R. M. Adams: 'Divine Command Metaethics Modified Again', *Journal of Religious Ethics*, vol. 7, 1979.

2. Cf. P. T. Geach: *Reference and Generality*, Cornell University Press, emended ed, 1968, p. 6 ff.
3. See his 'Abstract Objects', *Review of Metaphysics*, vol. XVI, 1964.
4. Bertrand Russell, 'On Denoting', *Mind*, 1905, repr. in *Logic and Knowledge*, R. C. Marsh (ed.), Allen & Unwin, 1956. See also John R. Searle, 'Proper Names', *Mind*, vol. 67, 1958; and his *Speech Acts*, CUP, 1969, ch. 7.
5. In 'Frege's Problem of the Morning Star and the Evening Star', *Studien zu Frege/Studies on Frege*, Matthias Schirm (ed.), Frommann-Holzboog Verlag, Stuttgart, 1976, vol. 2, p. 222. Also in 'Essentialism, Continuity, and Identity', *Synthese*, vol. 24, 1974, note 22, p. 356. Saul Kripke uses a similar argument in 'Naming and Necessity', *Semantics of Natural Language*, G. Harman & D. Davidson (eds), Reidel, 1972, p. 277; and in 'Identity and Necessity', *Identity and Individuation*, M. K. Munitz (ed.), New York University Press, 1971, pp. 156–7.
6. See 'Identity and Necessity' in M. K. Munitz (ed.), *Identity and Individuation*, New York University Press, 1971, p. 145.
7. See Gilbert Harman, 'An Introduction to "Translation and Meaning" ', in *Words and Objections*, D. Davidson and J. Hintikka (eds), Reidel 1975, pp. 14–15.
8. Cf. Jerome Shaffer:

    I do not see why statements cannot be made about non-existents. We can dream about them, think about them, and describe them, just as we can wait for them, hope to have them, and look for them. We can mention them, allude to or direct attention to them, and make reference to them. One thing we cannot do, of course is to *point* to them, and someone who thinks of mentioning, alluding or referring as a substitute for pointing will be puzzled as to how we can point to what does not exist. (Existence, Predication, and the Ontological Argument', *Mind*, vol. LXXI, 1962, p. 313)

9. See Hilary Putnam: 'The Meaning of "Meaning" ' in *Mind, Language, and Reality; Philosophical Papers*, vol. 2, CUP, 1975, and other papers in that volume.
10. In *Journal of Religious Ethics*, vol. 7, 1979, sections of which are repr. in *Divine Commands and Morality*, Paul Helm (ed.), OUP, 1981. References are to Helm.
11. See A. G. N. Flew, 'The "Religious Morality" of Mr. Patterson Brown', *Mind*, vol. LXXIV, 1965, pp. 580–1; also James Rachels: 'God and Human Attributes'; *Religious Studies*, vol. 7, 1971, repr. in Helm (ed.), *Divine Commands and Morality*, OUP, 1981.
12. Cf. R. M. Hare, ' "Nothing Matter" ' in *Applications of Moral Philosophy*, University of California Press, 1972, pp. 40–1 for the similarity between emotivism and intuitionism.
13. See Hare, 'The Practical Relevance of Philosophy' in *Essays on Philosophical Method*, Macmillan, 1972, esp. pp. 112–13.

5 SUBJECTIVITY AND OBJECTIVITY

1. Cf. James Rachels: 'God and Human Attributes', *Religious Studies*, vol. 7, 1971.
2. Cf. R. M. Hare: 'Some Confusions about Subjectivity'; in J. Bricke (ed.), *Freedom and Morality* (Lindley Lectures) University of Kansas, 1976, pp. 206–7, for a modification of views expressed in ' "Nothing Matters" ', pp. 43–5.

Index